Vicious Circles in Education Reform

Vicious Circles in Education Reform

Assimilation, Americanization, and Fulfilling the Middle-Class Ethic

Eric Shyman

ROWMAN & LITTLEFIELD
Lanham • Boulder • New York • London

Published by Rowman & Littlefield
A wholly owned subsidiary of The Rowman & Littlefield Publishing Group, Inc.
4501 Forbes Boulevard, Suite 200, Lanham, Maryland 20706
www.rowman.com

Unit A, Whitacre Mews, 26-34 Stannary Street, London SE11 4AB

British Library Cataloguing in Publication Information Available

Library of Congress Cataloging-in-Publication Data
Names: Shyman, Eric, 1979– author.
Title: Vicious circles in education reform : assimilation, Americanization, and fulfilling the middle class ethic / Eric Shyman.
Description: Lanham, Maryland : Rowman & Littlefield, 2016. | Includes bibliographical references.
Identifiers: LCCN 2016027101 (print) | LCCN 2016039846 (ebook) | ISBN 9781475827217 (cloth : alk. paper) | ISBN 9781475827224 (pbk. : alk. paper) | ISBN 9781475827231 (electronic)
Subjects: LCSH: Public schools—United States. | Education—Social aspects—United States. | Educational change—United States.
Classification: LCC LA217.2 .S576 2016 (print) | LCC LA217.2 (ebook) | DDC 371.010973—dc23
LC record available at https://lccn.loc.gov/2016027101

∞ ™ The paper used in this publication meets the minimum requirements of American National Standard for Information Sciences—Permanence of Paper for Printed Library Materials, ANSI/NISO Z39.48-1992.

Printed in the United States of America

For Lori, Nathan, and Lucas

Contents

Preface

Perhaps the reason behind the importance of this book is best explained by an excerpt of a narrative from a different book:

> By many accounts public schools are in trouble today. Grim stories appear daily in the media about violence, high dropout rates, and low test scores. Beyond such immediate concerns lies an uneasiness about purpose, a sense that we have lost our way. As the larger purposes that once gave resonance to public education have become muted, constituencies that at one time supported public education have become splintered and confused about what to do.[1]

The public school system is the prototypical institution of a democratic society, and the very means by which both the democratic ideal and its corresponding democratic practices can be engrained into the very fabric of the society itself. Following in the wisdom of some of the greatest educational philosophers of American education, such as John Dewey and Neil Postman, schools, and the process of schooling, is not to be regarded as preparation for society, but rather society itself. It is therefore unsurprising that virtually every relevant social narrative at a given time can be tied to school and education in one way or another.

This notion is the very purpose of this book, and the reason it has been written in the first place. As an educator, educationist, and father of two children, one who currently attends public school, and one who will in due time, my interest and passion for this topic is personal, professional, and scholar-activist oriented. This book will deal with the imperative notion of citizenship and fulfilling one's civic duty. While there are many ways in which fulfilling such duty can be achieved, the means by which I choose to fulfill mine is to continue being a main part of the discussion, and hopefully a provocative one, in order to contribute to the discussion's propagation.

The realm of schooling and education has always been political, as virtually all public institutions are apt to be, at least to some degree. However, it is not the political nature of the school system that is problematic. Indeed, all politics really are is a persistent discussion about the state of things.

While many arguments occur over the politics themselves, the deeper, more integral issue is missed: the real outplay of power and dominance. It is not the politics that are problematic, but rather the undue and unfair distribution of the power that politicians and elites themselves hold in the decision-making processes of public institutions. While at one point the American political system was, at least purportedly, intended to be one that was representative of the greater public, it has become a system that is far more imperious by the elite than reflective of the masses.

Indeed, the true purpose of the intention of the American republic and the larger American experiment is arguable, and has been argued by many learned scholars and writers upon a number of platforms throughout its history. This issue extends the scope of this book. However, outplay in the specific realm of schooling and education is the very basis of the current narrative.

It appears that contemporary American society is as divided as it has ever been, with one of the key issues of division involving the deep and dubious entanglement between the private funds of the corporate world and the very public decisions of the government. Indeed, American culture, society, and economy can be, and has been, adeptly described as neoliberal, even with the increasing representation of neoconservative politicians. Neoliberal, in this sense, refers to the liberal system of governing and markets rather than what is thought of as liberal political ideologies.

However, the extent of the depth and breadth of "freedom" in the "free" market is immensely suspect. This is the basis of what has become of education reform, with the power elites of the corporate world pulling the strings of the public policymakers, entirely offsetting the very nature of a democratic practice and approaching what is far better described as a corporate plutocracy shrouded by the rhetoric of a free-market system.

To put a more obvious visage on the narrative, this book was written primarily during the time of the 2016 presidential election fiasco (the outcome of which is not known at the time of this writing). While many Americans fall largely on two distinct sides of this issue, distilled into those supporting *radical* candidates like Donald Trump and Bernie Sanders and those supporting more *traditional* candidates like Hillary Clinton and, to some degree, Ted Cruz and Marco Rubio, the message in all of it is clear: the country and its politics are changing drastically, and there is a revolution that needs to be had. Which way this revolution will direct the country also remains yet unknown. Indeed, I have my own hopes and predictions as virtually every other American does as well.

Embedded in these fervent discussions, however, are more directed and focused social imperatives, among them being nativism versus xenophobia, centralization versus decentralization, and welfare-based practices versus individualistic pursuits. These are the very issues that can also be found at the heart of the education debate:

- Whether our country should use our schools to maintain and ensure American economic dominance or whether our efforts should be more focused on citizenship and global collegiality and collaboration.
- Whether our schools should reproduce the "classic" American ethic of individualism and capitalism or shift to a deeper understanding of collectiveness and cultural plurality, producing a new and deeper definition of what it means to be "American."
- Whether our school system should be controlled by larger, centralized agencies and held to distinct standards that are common across the country, or whether the federal government has gotten too large, meddlesome, and imperious in the area of schooling.

The current practice is clear, the future direction is not.

However, the plutocratic nature of the current system of schooling and education remains only a result of an overarching social problem, albeit a significant one. That is the depth of social and historical amnesia that has plagued, and continues to plague, any education reform efforts. While policymakers and politicians use the public schools and children, as their most dramatic staging areas and compelling players for its political charades, the public is being farther and farther marginalized, if not entirely eliminated from any input or latitude in the decision-making processes of the institutions that are supposedly funded by their own tax dollars. This is not a new issue, and can be traced as far back as the beginning of the school system's development itself.

This important observation is both the importance of and the goal for the book. By taking an honest, earnest, critical look at the history of the public school system and its almost simultaneous implementation of reforms, the true danger of social and historical amnesia will be demonstrated. Preserving ignorance of the past is a powerful tool of oppression as it disallows the public to see, without question, that what has been tried and failed before is being tried again in a virtually identical way, likely destined to also fail again.

The previous attempts did little for true education reform but much for expanding the political powers of the privileged few while virtually eliminating the powers of the public many. This is the same as the current outcome, but the level of profit being made during the current phase and the level of powerlessness of the public are unprecedented, and have all but concretized the control of public money by private investors who are then permitted to use it in order to personally profit, and profit handsomely, from its exploitation.

In order to effectively redeem itself from this deepening plutocracy, the public must become aware of its own history and, in the vein of Santayana, not repeat it. It is hoped that the readers of this book will be able to take away not only a deeper awareness of the history of education reform, but also a new interpretation of its cultural, political, economic, and social significance. Keeping history at the center of the discussion of policymaking is a powerful check that the public can maintain on those that are not working toward their interests, and use to preserve their own rightful power in their own society.

NOTE

1. David Tyack, *School*, p. 2.

Acknowledgments

There are many people to whom I owe tremendous gratitude for contribution to the production of this book. First and foremost, Tom Koerner, Carlie Wall, and Bethany Janka of Rowman & Littlefield Publishers, without whom publication would not be possible. I owe deep gratitude to my wife, Lori, and my two sons, Nathan and Lucas, whose patience with me through the writing process allowed me to complete my work sufficiently enough to be "all-present" during family time. Much appreciation goes to my mother, Wendy, late father, Paul, my sister and brother-in-law, Amanda and Michael, and my special nephew and niece, Reece and Ellery. Without family one has nothing. Last but not the least also to my loyal Dixie, whose quiet patience is always calming and conducive to writing and contemplation.

Scholastically, I owe much thanks to Dr. Elizabeth Finnegan, Dr. Susan Voorhees, and Dr. Edgar Daniels whose suggestions, critique, conversation, and feedback on earlier versions of this book, as well as its underlying ideas, contributed significantly to its betterment during the writing process. A second nod to Dr. Daniels, my colleague, office-mate, and friend, whose ever-stimulating conversations play a vital role in my writing and thinking process, is also in order.

To all of the incredibly astute, prolific, and daring intellectuals who came before me, and on whose shoulders I stand, who are too numerous to mention. Without curiosity, intellect, and constant questioning of the status quo, progress is simply not possible. Finally, to my students, past, present, and future who continue to teach more than I can ever teach them, and keep me motivated and dedicated to the field I love so deeply and dearly, education.

Introduction

The timeframe within which this book was first conceptualized and its writing began was likely among the most polarized periods in the nation's history (and most certainly in the author's lifetime). The preceding decade had brought to light the depth of the racial and ethnic tensions that continued to seethe within the bowels of American culture and society, and the myth of the "post-racial" America, signified by many by the election of President Barack Obama, the first black American president, was all too obviously shattered by the events that transpired during the second decade of the century such as the multiplicity of police shootings of young black men and women and the deepening xenophobia directed toward Muslims and Mexicans. Indeed, Americans on all sides of this issue wallowed in disappointment with the nation's progress and expressed that disappointment in their own way.

Politically, what had at one time been regarded as the far right had been transformed into moderate conservatism, marked by revolutionary sentiments from the emerging Tea Party's members such as Ted Cruz. Responses from the far left were increasingly present as well, especially with the advent of the first presidential candidate who openly declared himself a "democratic socialist," Bernie Sanders. Regardless of where on the political and ideological spectrum one fell, it was clear that the American public was in an extreme state of unrest and would tolerate little more of the status quo. The public had not only lost its power, but had lost its identity to an overpowering, if not despotic, elite.

The state of education was microcosmic of this notion. While the long history of educational unrest will be revealed to go back as far as the public school system itself, if not even farther, the unrest reached a critical mass during the years of 2001 through 2016, and will likely continue beyond them. What was once regarded as America's most sacred public institution,

1

the public school system, was not only under political and social attack, but it was, quite literally in many cases, being usurped and commoditized by the private corporate system. American schools were in the throes of the most significant "overhaul" in its history, and members of the public representing all social facets, including education experts, were relegated to be virtually powerless in their ability to intervene.

Vicious Circles in Education Reform will attempt to retell the public school system narrative in an original way and apply an original interpretation. By situating the narrative within a historicism perspective, the significance of not only events, but how those events both reflected and reformed the culture itself will be examined through a sociopolitical lens. Instead of relating only facts and events that occurred throughout the development of the public school system, these facts will be presented squarely within its sociocultural context, revealing a history of cultural vicissitudes that has struggled persistently with forging its own identity as well as finding its true value system while remaining accessible, at least in theory, to a wide variety of citizens.

Indeed, the centrality of schooling, or at least education of some sort, has ever been central to the concept of the American experiment, for better or worse. As Tyack suggests, "One article of faith among the founding fathers was that a republic could survive only if its citizens were educated. School has continued to shape the core of our [national] identity."[1] As the subsequent narrative will reveal, it is the proprietorship of that schooling process, not the importance of it, that will create the most tension and unease among those whose mission it was to be sure of its existence. This unease continues contemporarily.

Perhaps the most significant challenge of what has become of America's public school system is its centricity as both the source of and the solution to virtually all of America's social problems and issues. The state of the nation's education system has been cause for both celebration and degradation. It has been the site of political initiatives intended to bolster the campaign promises of particular elected officials as well as the means by which presidents and federal administrations have displayed their undying sense of nationalism and pride in the supreme talent of American youth.

Conversely, it has been the victim of intense derision, used to signal the degradation of American society, the American ideal, and its potentially questionable future. It has been tied to the country's economic and cultural survival, and used as a threat to its very national security. Indeed, the schools have been a veritable magnet for amplifying larger social commentary. It is through the schools alone that the youth and adult members of America are expected to collaborate and come to an understanding of not only what it *means* to *be* American, but to put these thoughts and sentiments into action.

As Tyack further suggests:

Achieving a sense of common purpose has never been easy. For two centuries public school districts have been political arenas in which citizens have contended with one another. In a society as socially diverse as the United States, controversies about purposes and practices in public schools are hardly surprising. Such policy debates express both hopes and fears about the nation. When citizens deliberate about the education for the young, they are also debating the shape and the future for the whole nation.[2]

No doubt, schools are important, if not central, to America's identity and survival. But what is at the core of the debate that goes on in America's schools? Tyack indicates it quite clearly. The major issue of contention in the area of public schooling is twofold. First is the issue of what the purpose of schooling truly is. That is, is it for making the citizen, or making the worker? Second is who gets to decide this purpose. Is it entirely in the hands of the public, the experts, the various interdisciplinary boards on which the system relies, or those who are in power to make and implement policy regardless of their expertise or true involvement? It is on these two questions that the history of the formation of the public schooling system itself and its almost entirely simultaneous history of reform center.

What this narrative will show then, though somewhat complex in its analysis, is quite simple in its main conclusion. While many descriptions of the public school system and its corresponding reforms have been described as pendulous, this metaphor proves less than apt at describing what truly happens in these periods of putative reform. While the operation of the metaphor lies in the "swing" of the proverbial pendulum, that is, it swings one way, and then swings back, there is found a notion of progression as well as regression. That is, as the pendulum moves forward, there is progression, while as it swings backward, there is regression.

This is not likely the case. Rather, the notion of the vicious circle is far more apt at capturing the movement of education reform. The vicious circle refers to the notion that contentious actions by one party evoke retaliatory or contentious action from another leading to further development of mutual negative perceptions between the parties.[3] The discussion itself, as well as the reform initiatives, has been entirely circular, with elements of both progression and regression evident in all elements of the initiatives, leaving the system itself virtually stagnant. Given the notion that the goal of reform is to get to the metaphorical center of the circle, the history tells a story of the system not improving and then worsening, but never quite getting anywhere, remaining equally as far from the center of the circle as it's always been, just maintaining the distance from different stances, perspectives, and destinations.

There are a number of potential explanations for this stagnation, many of which will be grappled with in the book. Chapter 1 will address the importance of narratives, and establishing historical and social narratives to begin with. Indeed, it is the narrative itself that shapes and propagates the culture, so the telling and retelling, interpretation and reinterpretation, is the veritable blood of a surviving culture. Chapters 2 and 3 will attempt to address two of the more commonly held purposes of schooling; that is, one as a sorter of people and the other as an assimilator of "others."

Chapters 4 through 7 will closely examine the cultural elements of schooling and school reform such as the role of science, globalization, and control. Chapters 8 through 14 will give the narrative its ultimate shape by looking at how schools have historically marginalized, if not entirely excluded, groups of "others" who violated the middle-class ethic of what it is to be "American," most notably based on race, ethnicity, gender, socioeconomic status, native language, and ability.

Finally, chapter 15 will introduce some basic ideas that should be used to guide discussions on the future of education reform in America with the ultimate goal of focusing on citizenship instead of competitiveness, and uprooting the tight grasp that the exclusive, supremacist, and inequitable middle-class ethic has on the functionality of schools.

It is through this retelling and reinterpretation of the public school system's historical narrative that the notion of the vicious circle will be demonstrated; for what ultimate purpose, however? The answer to this question is clear. While the ultimate fulfillment of this purpose must drastically extend this, or any other single work, it is to contribute to the growth of the counter-narrative to the conformity focused and non-pluralistic basis of the current American educational system.

This narrative expansion works to progress the system toward one that does not simply provide ceremonious nods to historically and systematically marginalized groups such as Black History Month, "character education" initiatives, and inspirational and motivational guest speakers in auditorium based mass symposia, but rather to engrain the very nature of pluralism into its curricular fabric. This is the ultimate purpose of the critical voices in education.

NOTES

1. *Ibid*, p. 1.
2. *Ibid*, p. 2.
3. Lawrence A. Pervin. (2015). Goal Concepts in Personality and Social Psychology. New York: Psychology Press.

Chapter 1

The Stories We Tell
Narratives of Public Schooling

The American public schooling system as we currently know it has been in service for roughly 175 years. From its very inception, the notion of public schooling itself and the conflict and struggle that have surrounded it regarding its purpose, curriculum, qualification of teachers and administrators, frequency, and accessibility, among a myriad other issues, have been staggering. One truth remains clear, however: that the public school system represents one of the most foundational institutions of a democratic society, and that it will ever be a lightning rod for social, political, and ethical debate.

These debates percolate furiously, coalescing every so often into a widespread movement for public education reform. And while the concept of reform often connotes a movement toward political or social change of one form or another, a closer examination of the history of public schooling reform efforts tells a strange, repetitive, and cyclical tale vacillating between two general political ideas: the purpose of schooling as a preparatory ground for work and economic contribution, and the purpose of schooling as a preparatory ground for citizenship and civic contribution.

While there is no true need for these two concepts to be regarded as mutually exclusive, it appears that they have, indeed, remained largely as such in the historical struggles over the American public schooling system. And, when appearing together (as they have in certain contexts of current discussions on education reform) the value of one (economic contribution) is clearly placed farther above the other despite the inclusion of both concepts in the general rhetoric.

This chapter will closely examine the historical development of both the American public schooling system as an institution. More deeply, it will then explore the connection between the public schools themselves and the greater social and political concerns that have been reflected in its processes over the last four centuries. What will be demonstrated is that, from its very inception, the American public schooling system was, and remains, a largely ideological experiment which serves as one of the most telling and accurate instruments for disseminating dominant social and political narratives and, in one way or another, handles the various counter-narratives that are told in its opposition.

It will further be demonstrated that instead of a system which possesses policymakers who have learned from past policymaking efforts and have progressively repaired and revised their approaches to various educational policy challenges through such reflection, the American public schooling system seems to have been doomed to a largely vicious circle of familiar rhetoric and myopic reform efforts, most of which has led to little, if any, true amelioration.

The central component upon which this chapter relies is that of history, and the important role that history plays in continuing toward a constructive and productive conversation about education reform. As the educational theorists and historians Larry Cuban and David Tyack suggest:

> Anyone who would improve schooling is a captive of history in two ways. All people and institutions are the product of history ... and ... all people use history (defined as an interpretation of past events) when they make choices about the present and future.[1]

Further, a study of history allows participants of a culture to revisit its own past, albeit often through a likely confusing and distorting lens that almost always proves to superimpose contemporary notions on past events, in order to discern whether its cultural memory is, indeed, accurate; that is, whether the culture's "way" has been lost, or whether it has never really been found to begin with. As Tyack suggests further:

> Perhaps one reason many Americans feel that we have lost our way in education is that we have forgotten where we have been. Reformers often say that amnesia is a virtue when it comes to reinventing education. The problem with that stance is that it is impossible. Everyone uses some sense of the past in everyday life, and leaders cannot escape thinking in time. The real question is whether the histories we all use in decision making enrich and ground understanding of the choices we make.[2]

This chapter will begin the telling, or perhaps more aptly the original retelling of the history of American public education from an interpretive interdisciplinary perspective. This retelling will serve as the grounding for constructive, productive, and fruitful discourse about the potential positive future of genuine education reform, one which is not held prisoner by super-imposing ideologies and reinterpretations of the past, but rather a sort of anthropomorphized version that can use the knowledge of its own past to not be "doomed to repeat it," in the vein of Santayana. As Katz suggests, current academic study attempts to

> expand notions of social, cultural, intellectual, and political development through exploring and highlighting the role of education in modern history. The work on education, at its best, however, has not been simply the reflex of social history, plugging schooling into the framework erected by scholars in more academically established specialties, but, rather, a catalyst which itself has forced the expansion of interpretations and the re-opening of historical issues.[3]

When attempting to address an institution as leviathan and protean as the American public school system, it is common to attempt to adhere to one of two fallacies: (1) either that the school system has lost sight of the practices that existed in some "golden age" of America's past, or (2) that schools have never truly captured the essence of American culture to begin with. While both are widely cited as explanations for the failure of American public schooling in many frames, the likelihood remains that the veracity of such a dichotomous distinction is ultimately impossible. Indeed, a reading of history of public schooling reveals that there were elements of education that were indicative of positive and effective instructional practices as well as aspects of American culture that were effectively captured and conveyed in schools at any given time.

This is not the important question, however. The important question, likely twofold, is whether or not those practices that appeared to be effective and those essential aspects of American culture that were captured did, indeed, effect the necessary change in American society in order to make it a positive contributor to the ever-growing global society, and whether schools alone can and should be held responsible for such a task. According to Ravitch:

> Probably no other idea has seemed more typically American than the belief that schooling could cure society's ills ... Americans have argued for more schooling on the grounds that it would preserve democracy, eliminate poverty, lower the crime rate, enrich the common culture, reduce unemployment, ease the assimilation of immigrants to the nation, overcome differences between ethnic groups, advance scientific and technical progress, prevent traffic accidents, raise health standards, refine moral character, and guide young people into useful occupations.[4]

Neil Postman calls the question even more directly:

> What are schools for? Schools are to fashion Americans out of the wretched refuse of teeming shores. Schools are to provide the lost and lonely with a

common attachment to America's history and future, to America's sacred
symbols, to its promise of freedom. The schools are, in a word, the affirmative
answer to the question, "can a coherent, stable, unified culture be created out of
people of diverse traditions, languages, and religions?"[5]

Through the examination of the development of the American public
school system, we find copious examples, ideas, and stories regarding what
public schooling should do, for what it is responsible, what elements should
comprise its curricula, and who should make such decisions, among the
panoply of other essential aspects of the American educational institution.
The question seemed never to be, at least since the founding fathers took on
the issue earnestly, *whether* schools are necessary. Rather, the true thrust of
the problem begs one basic question: What are the purposes of American
public schools?

But how do the purposes of an institution such as public education become
established and conveyed? How are they determined as to which aspects of
the culture are valuable enough to impart, held as essential to the very existence and propagation of the culture, and which should be stymied? And is
it a conscious, deliberate decision on the part of curriculum designers or do
schools merely reflect the dominant perceptions of the culture at a given time?

The essence of the problem becomes one of narrative: how narratives are
created, conveyed, and applied in the practice of cultures. That is, what are
the competing narratives that vie for influence in the planning, operation, and
purpose fulfillment of public schooling? And how is it determined which ones
prevail, becoming the dominant narrative, and which ones wane, becoming
the marginalized counter-narratives? For any solely human-made institution
such as public schools, an unceasing narrative is not only essential for its
inception and creation, but also for its propagation. As Neil Postman further
suggests:

> Our [humans'] genius lies in our capacity to make meaning through the cre-
> ation of narratives that give point to our labors, exalt our history, elucidate the
> present, and give direction to our future ... the purpose of a narrative is to give
> meaning to the world, not to describe it scientifically ... we are unceasing in
> creating histories and futures for ourselves through the medium of narrative.
> Without a narrative, life has no meaning. Without meaning, learning has no
> purpose. Without a purpose, schools are houses of detention, not attention.[6]

Narrative, according to Postman, is absolutely essential to the very function of public schooling not only to fulfill its academic and social duties, but
also to meet the cultural demands of a mercurial and mutable society such
as America's has always been and is likely to always be. The narrative, to
Postman, is the cornerstone of a public education that is to be cohesive and

unifying, disrupting the tendency for diverse societies to become splintered and segregated:

> [T]he idea of public education depends absolutely on the existence of shared narratives *and* [italics in original] the exclusion of narratives that lead to alienation and divisiveness. What makes public schools public is not so much that the schools have common goals, but that the students have common gods. The reason for this is that public education does not serve a public. It *creates* [italics in original] a public. And in creating the right kind of public, the schools contribute toward strengthening the spiritual base of the American creed.[7]

In the early republic it seemed clear that schooling was regarded solely as the responsibility of the church and, in other cases, the individual family, as schools primarily served to propagate the spiritual tenets of particular denominations. Therefore, in order to maintain the foundation of the separation between church and state, which was so fundamental to the basic tenets of the founding fathers, schools were kept entirely independent from the purview of government.[8] Thomas Jefferson and John Adams, however, regarded schooling (or education) in quite a different light than the prevailing opinion of their greater contemporary society.

As a true believer in an anti-tyrannical government of the people (albeit, one in which said government was run by representatives of the people as a republic, so as to keep the "great beast" tamed[9]) Adams maintained the essentiality of an educated public in that

> wherever a general knowledge and sensibility have prevailed among the people arbitrary government and every kind of oppression have lessened and disappeared in proportion. ... Orders of men, watching and balancing each other, are the only security; power must be opposed to power, and interest to interest ... religion, superstition, oaths, education, laws, all give way before passions, interest and power, which can be resisted only by passions, interest and power. ... The whole people must take upon themselves the education of the whole people, and must be willing to bear the expenses of it. There should not be a distance of one mile square without a school in it. Not founded by a charitable individual, but maintained at the public expense of the people themselves.[10]

As it turns out, Adams's perspective not only became a fundamental tenet of the later public schools movement, but bears an uncanny prescience of the 20th- and 21st-centuries struggles between private influences in public schooling, a central issue in current education reform discussions. Adams's insistence on the schools being a product of not only public expense but engrained within the public communities is a testament to the notion that, in Adams's vision, schools were not to be regarded as merely institutions in which technical skills and decontextualized knowledge are imparted to receptive students. Rather, schools are to be dynamic institutions within which one's civic responsibilities to one's society are truly and deeply cultivated.

The foundation of that process is to maintain not only the democratic ideal itself but also the self-preservation of the truly democratic society, disallowing any degree of tyranny to breach the fortress of the educated citizenry, which is not only obligated, but also dedicated to maintaining its will.

Jefferson, too, characterized schools as the central institution of the preservation of freedom as well as protection from the insidious power of hereditary aristocracy. As he declares:

> To enable every man to judge for himself what will secure or endanger his freedom. ... If we think [the people] not enlightened enough to exercise their control with a wholesome discretion, the remedy is not to take it from them, but to inform their discretion by education.[11] ... Education generates habits of application, of order, and the love of virtue; and controls, by the force of habit, any innate obliquities in our moral organization.[12]

What Jefferson suggests here is that education is the true antidote to a hereditary aristocracy that preserves classes and privilege based on bloodline rather than talent and skill. In this sense, Jefferson's ideas are similar to those of Plato, whose belief in an educated class was paramount to the preservation of a democratic society.

Seconding Adams's idea of schooling, to Jefferson, is a vivacious place of social action and cultural interaction, not a passive institution of knowledge reception and vocational training. Jefferson believed in this concept so deeply that he put forth a bill titled "Bill for the More General Diffusion of Knowledge" to the Virginia legislature three times between 1779 and 1817, which failed on each occasion, thus reinforcing the era's prevailing notion that the government should not be involved in the schooling process. As he offers an impassioned endorsement of it in a letter to George Wythe, his former professor at William & Mary:

> For the diffusion of knowledge among the people, no other sure foundation can be devised for the preservation of freedom and happiness ... preach, dear sir, a crusade against ignorance; establish and improve the law for educating the common people. Let our countrymen know that the people alone can protect us against these evils.[13]

This interpretation of the socially conscious and active purpose of schooling was not isolated to the central founding fathers; other influential leaders in the nascent republic, including Dr. Benjamin Rush and Noah Webster, forwarded efforts in their own respective states in order to strengthen the concept of public schooling. However, there has ever been a friction between Americans who were dubious of too much governmental power, state or federal, and Americans who believed in governmental regulation of the public realms, which was to eventually include the public school system. Though this conflict represented itself significantly as far back as the drafting sessions of the Constitution and the first meeting of the Senate and House of Representatives in 1789 as one of the fundamental rifts between the Federalists and the Antifederalists, it has taken on many forms and has applied itself to many issues throughout the centuries.

Given the prevailing opinion of education as localized, most formal schools that had been established from the early days of the new republic onward were largely decentralized, locally controlled institutions entirely independent from one another. The only remotely public aspect for some of these schools was the fiduciary contribution required of some parents for the running of the institutions. However, these fee-like payments were far from systematic or regulated in any way outside of local jurisdictions, and acted more as tuition than proper taxation. Even during Horace Mann's legislative call for better state regulation and funding of public schooling in the 1840s, he was met with widespread opposition from citizens who were wary of allowing any governmental involvement in an entity such as schooling.

During the mid-19th century such skepticism regarding any governmental influence in schooling was largely maintained, most likely due to the propagated function of religious groups and the family maintaining the responsibility for education. Because schools were seen as sacred spaces, of sorts, within which spiritual doctrine, religious values, and moral guidance were provided, the bastion of church and state was seen as strongly applicable to it. The very fact that federal funds were not spent on schooling on any significant scale until the early 1960s, and in a vastly significant way until Johnson's Great Society, indicates the very pervasive sentiment that schooling should be a localized entity that should be free of any governmental influence.

Even with the expansion of the government to include a Department of Education in 1979, which was to be led by a distinct Secretary of Education, the legislative language was careful to stipulate that the Department had limited governmental latitude:

> No provision of a program administered by the Secretary or by any other officer of the Department shall be construed to authorize the Secretary or any such officer to exercise any direction, supervision, or control over the curriculum, program of instruction, administration, or personnel of any educational institution, school, or school system, over any accrediting agency or association, or over the selection or content of library resources, textbooks, or other institutional materials by any educational institution or school system, except to the extent authorized by law.[14]

Additionally Congress, upon approving the establishment of the Department, made clear that the new agency does not supersede the role of state and local governments in matters of education.[15] The initiative came with much backlash and received much admonition from a variety of voices in government. Mary Berry, then assistant secretary for Education in the Department of Health, Education, and Welfare (the ancestral organization from which the Department of Education would be formed), insisted that

> [the role of the federal government in education] has and must continue to be a secondary role—one that assists, not one that directs local and State governments, which have historically shouldered the primary responsibility.[16]

In the statement proffered by the Dissenting Views of Representatives, the faction emphatically warned:

> This reorganization ... will result in the domination of education by the Federal Government ... [it is] a major redirection of education policymaking in the guise of an administrative reorganization—a signal of the intention of the Federal government to exercise an ever-expanding and deepening role in educational decision making.[17]

This position seems to have been prophetic, as similar sentiments have been expressed regarding the contemporary Race to the Top initiative (RTT) under the Obama administration. RTT was a competitive, multi-state grant that legislated availability of roughly $4.5 billion for education improvements to selected states that were chosen based on a number of criteria. One of these criteria was the adoption of rigorous content standards, a set of which was made conveniently available and incentivized through the Common Core State Standards (CCSS), a nongovernmental and corporation-backed product of a financially well-supported "education reform" project.

Many policymakers and government officials were wary of this effort for much of the same reasons asserted roughly 30 years prior to the establishment of the Department of Education. In 2009, then Commissioner of the Texas Education Agency Robert Scott wrote in a letter of concern to Senator John Cornyn:

> I believe that the true intention of [the Common Core Standards Initiative] is to establish one set of national education standards and national tests across the country. Originally sold to the states as voluntary, states have now been told that participation in national standards and national testing would be required as a condition of receiving federal discretionary grant funding under the American Recovery and Reinvestment Act (ARRA) administered by the [Department of Education]. ... With the release of the [Race to the Top] application, it is clear that the first step toward nationalization of our schools has been put into place.[18]

Indeed, the admonitions of those opposed to the establishment of the Department of Education appear to be taking hold, and the line between federal, state, and local control over education is quite apparently being blurred, if not entirely eliminated through the manipulative use of competitive grant money pitting the public systems of each state against one another, leading only to the possibility of an unequal, or even unfair, distribution of federal money for schooling.

NOTES

1. David Tyack and Larry Cuban, *Tinkering Toward Utopia: A Century of Public School Reform* (Cambridge, MA: Harvard University Press, 1997), 5.

2. David Tyack, cited in Sarah Mondale, *School: The Story of American Public Education* (New York: Beacon), 3.

3. Michael B. Katz, "The Origins of Public Education: A Reassessment." *History of Education Quarterly*, 16 no. 4, (1976), 381.

4. Diane Ravtich, *The Troubled Crusade*: *American Education 1945–1980* (New York: Basic Books, 1985), xii.

5. Neil Postman, *The End of Education: Redefining the Value of School* (New York: Vintage, 1996), 14.

6. Ibid., 7.

7. Ibid., 18.

8. Michael Roth, *Beyond the University: Why Liberal Education Matters* (New Haven, CT: Yale University Press, 2015).

9. Noam Chomsky, *Hegemony or Survival: America's Quest for Global Dominance* (New York: Holt, 2004).

10. Roth, *Beyond the University,* 23–25.

11. Ibid., 25.

12. Ibid., 30.

13. Ravitch, *The Troubled Crusade,* xi.

14. Section 103[b], Public Law 96–88. Retrieved from http://www2.ed.gov/about/overview/focus/what_pg4.html.

15. Robert S. Eitel and Kent D. Talbert, "The Road to a National Curriculum: The Legal Aspects of the Common Core State Standards, Race to the Top, and Conditional Waivers." *Engage,* 13 no.1, (2012): 13–25.

16. Ibid.

17. Ibid.

18. Ibid.

Chapter 2

Schooling as Sieve

Distinguishing between the Classes

Once the Industrial Revolution took hold in the late 19th century, a vast social change in the landscape and demographics of America's burgeoning cities ushered in. This social and economic change yielded perhaps the most significant deepening separation between the functions and demographic composition of urban and rural areas. As a result of this swift growth in urbanization the problem of schooling became a distinctly more relevant and exigent discussion in greater American society, leading to what would eventually become likely the first widespread education reform movement in American public schooling.

Interestingly and importantly, this initial reform movement occurred almost simultaneously with the development of the public schooling system itself. That is, the ideas of public schooling and its corresponding purposes had been clearly present in American society since the beginning of the republic, though the system itself was not, and these two inseparable but often antagonistic projects were to begin a long and still unresolved development spanning three centuries (and likely continuing).

With the increased interest in the quality of developing schools, which were still largely locally controlled, some systematic study of schooling as a discipline was present early in the 20th century. While at the time, the effect that the Industrial Revolution would have on child and youth labor was yet to be known, an emerging intellectual area, which would come to be known as *social science,* would begin its development and, as a result, an increased attention to and discussion of the nature of school curricula began to occur within America's universities. Specifically, a group of thinkers (who will later be discussed under the moniker of *mental disciplinarians*) gained immense popularity in the discussion involving curriculum design beginning in the mid-18th century.

Expressed systematically for the first time in the catalyzing Yale Report of 1828, the main focus for curriculum, according to the mental disciplinarians, should be that of the "classic" education: Greek, Latin, Mathematics, and Literature. These, the mental disciplinarians claimed, were the most efficient at strengthening the essential mental faculties such as memory, will, reason, and imagination—cognitive abilities that were highly valued by American culture at the time. In the view of the mental disciplinarians, the mind was to be viewed quite literally as a muscle, which was to be strengthened through mental drilling, harsh discipline, and verbatim recitation of "rules." This frame of thought largely influenced curriculum design from the late 19th century into the first quarter of the 20th century.

The framework of mental discipline did not only influence curriculum design, however. It also grounded the functionality of the school system even when the mental disciplinarians' philosophies of curriculum began to be challenged by other modes of thinking, as it was toward the end of the 19th century and early 20th century, most likely in direct response to the ever-increasing industrialization of America.

The prevailing counter-philosophy, eventually known as social efficiency, sought to establish schools and the schooling process into a sieve of sorts. That is, in addition to schools becoming institutions in which curricula are delivered in order to "strengthen the mind," schools became the site at which the process of "sorting" students in a system that was deeply based in classism took place. Essentially, this consisted of eliminating the "undesirables" from formal education through alternative pathways and redistributing them to the service or vocational fields where they would train to be wage earners or tradesmen.

This system was predicated on the already existent and deep-seated hereditarily aristocratic notion that education and the "white collar" professions were intended for a privileged class, while service in the more manual "blue collar" professions was intended for the rest of the society, a notion that was explicitly opposed by Adams, Jefferson, Emerson, and DuBois, as well as a myriad other foundational American thinkers both before and since. The validity of social efficiency theory was supported through various inquiry endeavors in what would eventually be seen as early examples of educational research.

In 1913, for example, Helen Todd, a factory inspector, interviewed youth in factory jobs and determined that they did not leave school out of economic necessity, but rather because the curriculum and methodology at schools were "monotonous, humiliating, and cruel" and that a life of manual work was far more desirable.[1] Therefore, without the social or familial pressure to remain in school despite its adverse conditions or the child's general disinterest, those that were to become "workers" likely left, and those that were to retain their more privileged positions likely stayed, laying the groundwork for the American public school system to be built firmly upon the values of a generally privileged, and what to eventually become a more solidified middle class.

Ellwood Cubberley, dean of the Stanford School of Education vocally supported the popularizing notion that the mental disciplinarian approach to schooling was far too academic and socially and economically irrelevant to be maintained as the focus of American curricula. Instead he believed that the social efficiency theorists were correct in proposing that schools should, indeed, be the site of "social sorting" in an effort to keep the society and one's role in it clearly intact. As he suggested:

> We should give up the exceedingly democratic idea that all are equal and that our society is devoid of classes. The employee tends to remain an employee; the wage earner tends to remain a wage earner ... one bright child may easily be worth more to the National Life than thousands of low mentality.[2]

With many supporting statements such as this, especially those among the policy elite who were gaining ever-growing influence on the school system due to the increasing enmeshing of private wealth with public governance, the connection between economic success and school purpose was deeply, if not indelibly, established.

From this social phenomenon, the foundational culture and basic tenets of American public schooling were established quite securely as an outcrop of middle- to upper-middle-class society, and was framed quite intentionally upon the values of that sector of the society. These values are, in all of the most foundational ways, still those that firmly guide both educational practice and policy, and can be seen as one of the major contributors of not only what will come to be called the "achievement gap," but also the very dichotomous and very real nature of the educational "haves" and "have-nots."

The popularizing conception of Social Darwinism, as propagated by Herbert Spencer in 1892, suggested that the laws that Darwin had declared as being foundational in terms of biological survival were also applicable as social laws, and the unequal distribution of wealth and liberty was to be seen simply as an immutable and natural application of that law within the realm of economics and society. This idea can be seen as a direct overlay to the dominant philosophy that guided social efficiency theory and, thusly, was engrained in American public schools simultaneously with the growing influence of social efficiency educational practices.

As Kliebard suggests:

> The route between the knowledge a society values and its incorporation into the curriculum becomes infinitely more tortuous, however, when we take into

account the fact that different segments in any society will emphasize different forms of knowledge as most valuable for that society. Rarely is there universal agreement as to which resources of a culture are the most worthwhile.[3]

Kliebard's astute point leaves little doubt that there is an indelible connection, if not direct influence, between the hegemonic culture and the curriculum of that culture's schools, leaving it stood to reason that such hegemonic messages and means of preservation would be embedded directly within the curricula and culture of America's public schools. With the exceedingly speedy growth of public schooling, as demonstrated by only 6–7 percent attendance in 1890 to over 50 percent in 1930,[4] the role that the public school will come to play in the cultivation of youth culture and the very definition of such foundational concepts in the study of education such as knowledge, intelligence, schooling, teaching, and learning, among other phenomena, became vastly important, serving to complicate the ever-raging debate over how, and why, to school.

The argument as to whether schools were designed to breed "citizens" who had deep knowledge of their civic responsibilities or "workers" who could contribute economically to their society through skilled work of one type or another was beginning to emerge; there appeared to be no shortage of heated exchanges between sides, few of which represented any form of moderation or incorporation of the two, at least at the beginning. The growing American economy, however, and the perception of the ever-increasing need to distinguish between manual "workers" who provided the "brawn" and political "managers" who provided the "brains" catapulted the perspective of schools as sieves and its supporting social efficiency paradigm into practical and curricular relevance.

Thus, the popular view had, indeed, become that schools were to provide "education according to the predicted social and vocational role"[5] of each student. This idea became so endemic to the purpose of schooling that it was soon deemed necessary for all activities completed in schools to be aligned with a specific industrial or vocational purpose.

This connection was fully realized when the principles of Frederick Winslow Taylor, considered the "father" of the scientific management of factories, were adapted to schooling administration and management, principally by Edward A. Ross and John Franklin Bobbitt, both of whom adopted industrial based epithets to describe the burgeoning public schools, such as regarding schools as "plants" and students as "platoons."[6]

This new amalgamation of the industrial and corporate importance of particular modes of teaching and curriculum would prove to be one of the most influential, if not nefarious, developments for American public schooling. This merge in approaches indelibly linked economic value and contribution to the availability of quality public schooling, as well as maintained a largely predetermined though ostensibly permanent classification system comprised of but a few societal conduits into which one was fit. This means of categorization, known in some contexts as "tracking," soon became a staple of educational practice in American schools.

According to Kliebard, schools in the first quarter of the 20th century were to be seen as "a new system of education tied to the 'callings of life' ... professional, commercial, productive, and domestic."[7] This link between schooling and economic productivity was already so deeply engrained in educational thought that as early as 1906 Helen Todd, the aforementioned factory inspector, declared that "our cloths can [now] compete with the foreign market" with proper training, a clear vote of approval for the new role of schooling as a training ground for vocation and its tie to global competitiveness, a concept which, to be sure, is to grow in significance over the proceeding century.

Not much later, in 1909, Leonard Ayres published *Laggards in Our Schools*,[8] which was to be an early example of the critical study of the economics of schooling, specifically in terms of for whom economic investment in education is best suited and most worthwhile. In this report, which was generated by studying school spending documents, not schooling practices directly, Ayres declared that roughly $27 million were "wasted" each year on curricula that were not fit for the "slow child." The process of sorting established in the late 19th century through the first quarter of the 20th century would lay some of the most significant groundwork for the future discriminatory social roles to be played by schools, and inarguably deeply remain in current schooling practices.

In this sense, the framework for American public schooling grew largely out of the overarching concept of economic capitalism, which was gaining dominance as a result of the Industrial Revolution and functioning inexorably within the public school system by the first quarter of the 20th century. This managerially based perspective, seen as a central tenet of the capitalistic paradigm, was an essential component of the capitalist system's appeal and an early example of the notion that schools, in essence, merely mirror dominant thought and value systems in its processes rather than effect social or cultural change. As Katz suggests:

> Public education received popular assent at least partly because it did not differ from the dominant ideology of democratic capitalism in nineteenth century North America. Public educational systems crystallized key components of social ideology into an institutional form and assured its transmission. The school system became a miniature version of the social order. Within both school and society, according to the ideal which underlay their organization, universalistic and individualistic criteria replaced the handicaps of birth, and

achievement became available on the basis of ability. Within the public schools, as within society at large, the able should rise simply by virtue of their own talents.[9]

Thus was the essential "battle cry" of capitalism which did not differ, in its purer, more original form, than those sentiments of Jefferson and Adams: that hereditary aristocracy was to be eliminated only by the establishment of an educated class, whose dominance was ascertained based on talent, not bloodline. These ideas, reminiscent of the "free market," were to serve an equalizing function. Essentially, based on this thinking, the public schools would foster a meritocracy, purportedly the most democratic of free systems, as according to the dominant social narrative of free-market capitalism.

Further, cultural assent of such a prevailing philosophy in public schools was a greater assent to such a philosophy in society as a whole. What more agreement would a society need than what was to become of the very institution that "trained" their children for the society of the future? However, a more deleterious aspect of this notion would also come to be inexorably engrained in schooling practices, and that is the deep and discriminatory system of classism, racism, sexism, ableism, heterosexism, and xenophobia (if not, more aptly, ethnicism).

Despite the economic and political endorsement of the social efficiency model of schooling, by 1925 there was a growing body of evidence that public schools were coming under harsh criticism not by the public who, according to polls, were shown to be generally satisfied with the public school system until the mid-1940s,[10] but by participants in the growing field of educational theory, a specialized branch of the ever-growing realm of social science. This early example of the passion with which various schools of thought fought for influence, if not control, over the public schools would be applicable for decades to come, and continues contemporarily.

At the heart of the debate was the omnipotent issue: the purposes of public schooling. That is, what was public schooling for? Was it to establish a sense of civic obligation and citizenship in its students? Was it to provide opportunities for the brain to receive its drills for development? Was it the institution in which students would learn what their social and economic roles would be beyond the school and begin training for that role? Was it some combination of these, or was it something else entirely? As it turns out, this question of purpose would remain at the heart of the education reform debate; it is yet to be resolved, and will likely never definitively be.

NOTES

1. Herbert M. Kliebard, *The Struggle for the American Curriculum: 1893–1958* (New York: Routledge, 2004).

2. Ellwood Cubberley, as cited by Sarah Mondale, *School: The Story of American Public Education* (New York: Beacon, 2002), 98.

3. Ibid., 7.

4. Ibid.

5. Ibid., 84.

6. Ibid.

7. Ibid., 86.

8. Leonard P. Ayres, *Laggards in Our Schools: A Study of Retardation and Elimination in City School Systems* (New York: Charities, 1909).

9. Katz, "Origins of Public Education," 401.

10. Tyack and Cuban, *Tinkering Toward Utopia*.

Chapter 3

Schooling and the *Real* America
Struggling toward Americanization

Though both mental disciplinarians and social efficiency theorists appeared to alternate the possession of the stronghold of American educational practice on the inchoate formal public school system, many great American thinkers shared the notions of Jefferson and Adams and, undoubtedly, disagreed with both of these eminent perspectives. As the prominent American thinker and essayist Ralph Waldo Emerson noted on the subject:

> What I must do is all that concerns me, not what the people think. This rule, equally arduous in actual and in intellectual life, may serve for the whole distinction between greatness and meanness. It is harder because you will always find those who think they know what is your duty better than you know it. It is easy in the world to live after the world's opinion; it is easy in solitude to live after our own: but the great man is he who in the midst of the crowd keeps with perfect sweetness the independence of solitude.[1]

With this Emerson prizes in the process of education the cultivation of individualized thinking. Indeed, even at the time of Emerson's writing there was already a deep-seated notion of content-based curriculum and the role of schooling as preserving and nurturing American society and culture rather than encouraging independent thinking.

W.E.B. DuBois, in response to the increasing prevalence of vocational training in schools (especially among black students in black schools), also provides a prescient and enduring admonition:

> If we make money the object of man-training, we shall develop money makers but not necessarily men; if we make technical skills the object of education, we may possess artisans but not, in nature, men. Men we shall have only as we make manhood the object of the work of schools—intelligence, broad sympathy,

23

knowledge of the world the way it was and is, and of the relation of men to it—this is the curriculum of that higher education which must underlie true life. On this foundation we may build bread-winning, skill of hand and quickness of brain, with never a fear lest the child and man mistake the means of living for the object of life.[2]

What is clear among the characterizations of the purpose of schooling from these deeply respected and influential American thinkers is that school is to be the site at which one's civic identity, civic duty, sense of citizenship, and sense of justice are to be nurtured and cultivated, as well as the site at which the student becomes prepared to continuously engage in such civic discourse and activity over his or her entire life. That is, the process of cultivating citizenship and civic duty does not end once formal schooling culminates, but rather schooling nurtures what will become the enduring reflective citizen who ever revisits the meaning and activity of his or her citizenship. Indeed, such activities of citizenship include one's economic contribution; but it is not limited to it, nor is it even among the most important outcomes.

It is these very ideas of citizenship and civic responsibility that will become the focal point of over a century of debate, discussion, and disagreement. It is important to note, however, that Emerson's viewpoints, as well as DuBois's (among a number of other purportedly socially influential people) effectively played little role in the decision making of political policymakers. This distinction is an early example of the separation between the influence of esteemed, erudite public intellectuals and powerful policy elites, which remains a foundational separation in the current political system, including public schooling.

From a philosophical standpoint, it can be argued that public schools were an outgrowth of the ever-growing influence of the Protestant-Republican ideology that had so invariably and inarguably shaped the policies of America from its very beginnings, despite the notional centrality of the separation of church and state. According to W.W. Carpenter, schooling is "furnishing to the youth of our land nobler temples in which their hearts, minds, and bodies may better adjust themselves to the demands of a practical civic brotherhood."[3]

But how did the school system itself come to be? While there were clearly elements of public schooling growing during the time of the new republic, the likely forebears of the current public school system were not evident until the mid-19th century, which would come to be known widely as "common schools." By the 1840s the value of literacy began to grow exponentially for three distinct reasons.

First, the growing presence of the Protestant movement and its influence on society encouraged people to read the Bible in order to gain a better understanding of morality as conceptualized by Scripture. Indeed, it was the Bible that underscored virtually all decision making, for better or worse, during this part of American history. Despite maintaining the nominal separation between church and state, the basis of Christianity, and particularly the Protestant brand, was a central frame of reference for political and social decision making.

Second, social unrest remained relatively common since the ratification of the Constitution, merely three-quarters of a century earlier. With the still somewhat new republic continuing to experience significant disagreements regarding the structure and purposes of the government itself, literacy became an integral means of disseminating matters of political and social importance through the publication of pamphlets and newspapers. The suffusion of these media was bolstered significantly by the growing availability of printing presses, increasing the value of the written word manifold.

Third, the pervading Protestant work ethic valued, quite emphatically, the development of a strong commercial and economic system, providing one of the main foundations for connecting schooling and economic contribution, which the social efficiency theorists would come to build upon at the beginning of the 20th century. Essentially, schools would become the very sources of teaching, reading and writing, and acting as a preparatory ground for future members of the economic community. Additionally, regular attendance of children at school would allow other family members who were already engaged in commerce to become more involved in the marketplace without the distraction of having to fulfill their caretaking duty for their children. This notion was to become a cornerstone of the growing capitalist value system, which had a significant effect on the growing and morphing American economy.

But as history would come to reveal, this upsurge in prosperity during the late 19th and early 20th centuries would be relatively temporary. In the 1930s, by the revealing light of the stock market crash and the worsening economic depression, legislation was passed to make high school attendance compulsory. While this legislative action is often couched in the context of the increased social value of schooling, the initiative was enacted primarily in order to relieve the already depressed job market of many able-bodied and less expensive youth workers, allowing more gainful employment opportunities for able-bodied men.[4]

However, as a more socially relevant result of the depression many public intellectuals, scholars, and even politicians began to take serious interest in how a society that was so deeply engrossed in economic concerns could refocus its efforts on investing in the society itself, as well as the citizen. Many sought such answers within the ideas and application of communism and socialism (or, perhaps more aptly Marxism), a frame of thought which was situated in direct opposition to capitalism, and one that was historically vilified by prototypical American culture and ideology.

Among the most vocal intellectuals to connect this emerging interest in socialism and communism to matters of education was George S. Counts, the famed Teachers College educational historian, as well as a number of his esteemed colleagues including John Dewey. This emerging group of American intellectuals operated from an anti-capitalist and pro-democratic standpoint, suggesting that democracy as a governing process must be disentangled with political structures in order to be fully realized and practiced.

Further, this viewpoint challenged the notion that democratic ideals were inseparable from an individualistic capitalistic economy, and that democracy could actually be better fulfilled within the framework of a collectivist socialistic one. Education, they believed, was the structure by which such change could be truly effected. As an article in *Social Frontier*, a socialist thought—centered Teachers College publication, declared:

> A collectivist social order has the promise of genuine freedom, an abundant, rich, colorful, socially significant life for the many where they now can find comfort only in an empty legalistic formula ... there can be no freedom of thought and expression ... [in] an economy based on private property in the means of production and private profits ... history has pronounced this verdict.[5]

However, despite this enclave being comprised of legitimate and respected scholars, their works would remain on the fringe largely as a result of their somewhat esoteric and academic handlings of complex issues, most of which proved inaccessible and, therefore, uninteresting to the general public. As a result there quickly spread disingenuous and largely bastardized versions of socialism and communism.

This perfusion of discussion reflected the genuine interest of the public in exploring collectivistic ideas, but betrayed their true understanding and application, resulting in ones that either overly romanticized true Marxism or remained ignorant to (if not intentionally ignore) the sheer brutality of what became Stalinism, if the two were not erroneously seen as entirely synonymous. The communist and socialist presence in America, then, was largely unsuccessful at effecting any meaningful social change in its favor, but remarkably adept at attracting harsh criticism, especially from a decidedly more politically powerful, capitalistic and wealthier conservative contingency.

One critical result of this interest in connecting socialism with education was the establishment of the first teachers union in 1916, chartered as a local chapter of the American Federation of Labor (AFL). Later, growing out of disagreements between communists and socialists within the union itself, the AFL chapter split and a separate branch called the Teachers Guild was established in 1935. This outgrowth of socialism among teachers was to become a deep-seated and oft-cited critique of teacher unions being communistic, anti-capitalist, and, ultimately, anti-American.

However, it is important to recognize that when the political degradation of the teacher unions is properly contextualized, the socialist roots of the organizations reveal not a legacy of "anti-Americanism" at all, but rather one of a questing for economic and social fairness in schools, an entirely American ideal, vying for a system that the capitalistic social efficiency models clearly did not (nor did they seek to) provide.

Despite the questionable success or effect of change brought about by increased intellectual interest in socialism or the pervasion of capitalist based social efficiency, especially among those involved with educational theory, an important phenomenon was revealed: that there was a deep, intractable common faith in the ability of the public schools to serve as a panacea for social ills. The notion that it is the school that is the source of both the propagation of cultural values and the amelioration of social problems is one that remains strong, if not indelible, in American society. This newfound faith represented a distinct shift in ideology from viewing social problems, and their ultimate handling, as a largely localized matter to the belief that formal, systemic institutions may be better apt to deal with such challenges.

Among a number of social problems facing growing American communities, especially urban areas, was migration and transiency. That is, with many immigrants and American-born citizens needing to move regularly in order to find work, the functions of communities, and even their very existence in some cases, began to erode. With such erosion came the increase in crime and poverty, cultural heterogeneity, the increase of an "unskilled" labor force, and the threat to the middle class regarding the social standing and opportunity for their own youth and adolescence.[6]

As a result, local and state governments, through the appendages of their bureaucracies, invested more heavily in establishing community schools in order to provide a physical space within which both wayward youth and "middle-class" youth alike could be contained for much of the day. It also provided a ground upon which both "classes" could become (or remain) civilized, potentially yielding the reduction in social decadence. Essentially, with local and state government investments, schools became an alternative to almshouses and jails at a much cheaper social and economic price.

In the mid-1940s, however, the beginning of a trend that would be cyclically observed in the realm of public schooling was outplayed for the first time. After the culmination of World War II, a deeper, more critical perspective of the American government began to emerge from multiple perspectives. Commensurate with the early beginnings of the Cold War with Russia, an increasing number of Americans expressed that they feared America's public schools were lagging behind other countries in terms of its ability to maintain competitiveness globally.

Epitomizing this belief was Russia's success with *Sputnik*, declaring them the clear "winners" of the "Space Race," at least initially. This "loss" engendered a generational mistrust that was to be maintained over multiple future generations, causing the older generation to question whether America had "lost its youth" and what the consequences of such a loss might be, while the younger generation questioned the ideals and values of their forefathers and attempted to forge a new, better, and more meaningful social path.

It is at this juncture that the fear of losing ground in the realm of global competitiveness easily couples with the notion of the need to regain the spirit and practices of "yesteryear" by launching an all-out assault on current American values and how they are conveyed in public schools. This preoccupation with "global competitiveness" is to become yet another clear trend in the catalyzing of educational reform. Essentially, the schools were seen as the locus at which radicalism of any kind could be squelched and capitalism and nationalism, or essential Americanism, could be reinvigorated and re-infused in the youth, thus securing a more prosperous and prideful American future. According to Ravitch:

> Educational institutions became focal points for large areas of consensus ... [as well as] magnets for dissension, attracting all those who wanted to change the social order, preserve threatened traditions, challenge historic wrongs, or make sure that the next generation was not tainted by the errors of their predecessors.[7]

This friction between socialism (and its resulting perception of "anti-Americanism") and capitalism (and its respective perception of "patriotism") took full form in the 1950s through the widespread practice of McCarthyism and the perception of the growing societal threat that American communists posed to the well-being of American democracy. This public hysteria cast greater suspicion on public schools, especially in light of increasing unionization of American teachers and its very real ties with socialism and socialist-based or socialist-leaning organizations. This suspicion caused many districts to resort to dubious practices in the name of securing nationalism and patriotism, thereby squelching any sense of "anti-American" practices in the schools.

By 1950 thirty-three states adopted legislation to oust disloyal teachers (teachers who were seen as "anti-Capitalist" or "anti-American" usually as a result of membership in a perceived socialist group such as an organized labor union), while twenty-six had adopted a "loyalty oath" requirement, a practice for which the constitutionality was upheld by the Supreme Court in 1952. Further, in 1952, Bella Dood prompted public hearings concerning the connection between the New York Teacher Union and communists, one of the main public occurrences that forever embroiled the battle against teachers within the battle against all things "un-American" and all but solidified the association between teacher unions and communism.

Gaining attention of the greater community, especially those of the elite, Albert Lynd, a businessman and school board member, published a report entitled *Quackery in the Public Schools*, an unapologetic invective against what he termed the "educationist monopoly," specifically those pedagogues operating from a Progressive vantage, who he claims usurped the schools from the rightful hands of the public (a clear euphemism for the corporate elite). A trend that was to be seen in increasingly deeper ways, this was one of the first indications of members of upper-class corporate America not only taking interest in and gaining influence of educational policy, but declaring "educationism" to be neither a science nor a discipline, but rather a charlatanic enterprise in need of little more than managerial business sense, no different than any other corporate style entity.

Effectively, Lynd suggested that schools were not dependent on educational expertise for success, but rather business and managerial acumen. In many ways, Lynd and his compatriots signaled the completion of the first vicious circle in American education reform. The circle, beginning with the mid-19th-century prominence of the mental disciplinarians who declared the mind as a muscle, to the usurpation of the oppositional social efficiency theorists who drew the first comparisons between schools and businesses, then replaced by the Progressives wary of capitalistic tendencies, who were again replaced by the conservative and suspicious interests of businesses and corporate elites reminiscent of the initial social efficiency theorists unwilling to lose America to communists and "quacks." This vicious circle was to be seen again and again in a variety of ways.

The notion of establishing a national identity is a deep tenet of Americanism that can be traced directly back to the Revolutionary War and those hallowed men we deem our "founding fathers." Indeed, many post-Revolutionary reformers believed that the very essence of liberation was education. Therefore, through the establishment of educational institutions the identity of a patently "non-British American" could be created, instilled, and preserved in its youth."

One clear example of such identity creation came in the form of Noah Webster's call to ban all British-created texts, as well as the creation of the "Webster's Speller," a precursor to the eponymous and soon ubiquitous dictionary. The "Webster's Speller" respelled all British-English words into a distinct "American-English" style, for example *music* as opposed to *musick* and *honor* as opposed to *honour*. Given the coming upsurge in the importance of written text, this exercise proved to be a fruitful one in distinguishing American English from that used by the British.

In the mid-18th century, a Minnesota-based publication proffered a similar sentiment in response to the increasing immigration from European countries:

[public schools] take the child of the exile of Hungary, of the half-starved emi-
grant from the Emerald Isle, and of the hardy Norwegian, and places them on
the same bench with the offspring of those whose ancestors' bones bleached
upon the field of Lexington. ... as the child of the foreigner plays with his school
fellow, he learns to whistle "Yankee Doodle" and sing "Hail Columbia" and
before he leaves the school-desk for the plough, the anvil or the trowel, he is as
sturdy a little republican as can be found in the land.[8]

However, despite this deep sense of the need for an American identity and
the value that education can have in establishing such an identity, schools
remained largely decentralized and unregulated until the 1840s when Horace
Mann, an influential legislator and businessman from Massachusetts, made
the issue of public schooling his political focus.

Based on a survey of several public schools, which, as the story goes, was
conducted on horseback, Mann was dismayed to find gross inequity between
the schools in privileged white neighborhoods and schools in poverty-ridden
black neighborhoods across the state of Massachusetts. Issues such as taxes
and private fees enabling wealthier white families to provide better schools
and the inconsistency between learning resources, materials, and even physical structures within which schooling was held led Mann to advocate for
the state regulation of public schools. This project came to be known as the
establishment of the "common school." According to Mann:

You crowd 40 to 60 children into that ill-constructed shell of a building, there to
sit in the most uncomfortable seats that could be contrived, expecting that with
the occasional application of the birch they will come out educated for manhood
and womanhood.[9]

According to Mann, the main purpose of education was to develop children's character, ubiquitously framed within the Protestant context. As a
result, Mann argued that there should not be a haphazard network of largely
independent sectarian schools offering disparate idiosyncratic teachings, but
rather a centralized system of schooling based on the main moral teachings
of the Bible. Some critical scholars interpret this imposition as adopting an
overarching framework of the common schools within the Protestant ethic,
essentially minimizing sectarianism only by virtue of unifying schools under
Protestantism.

In many respects the thrust of Mann's proposal was to depoliticize schools
by focusing on the central tenets of being "American," which were, to him,
inseparable from those tenets of being "Protestant" such as freedom, liberty,
and individuality. Hence, to be American is to be Protestant, and vice versa.
Attaining such an identity could be achieved only by presenting a glorified,
largely mythologized version of the founding fathers, thus creating and

perpetuating the narrative of a unified, patriotic, and ideologically grounded America with a clear national identity. This narrative, if presented in a "story-telling" manner, would be easy for schoolchildren to believe and, thus, internalize as the true story of their nation's history.

The result was a unified, largely unchallenged dominant curriculum upon which the central identity of being "American" (and thus "Protestant") could be constructed. As such, the common school was to serve both boys and girls alike, teach the common body of knowledge (all of which was based on the Protestant ethic), be free of charge to all members of the community, and not distinguish between rich and poor children in terms of physical and intellectual quality. In Mann's words:

> It is a free school system, it knows no distinction of rich and poor ... it throws open its doors and spreads the table of its bounty for all the children of the state. ... Education, beyond all other devices of human origin, is the equalizer of the conditions of men, the great balance wheel of the social machinery.[10]

Mann, in this sentiment, embraced that unique American ideal of the sanctity of the school as the source of great social change, and education as the means of lasting social melioration. However, despite Mann's apparent rhetoric of sectarianism and "Americanism" it is important to maintain the context of Mann's theories squarely within the Protestant ethic. As Ravitch reminds us:

> If you read Horace Mann you will see that his idea was we should have no sectarianism in the schools—we should all read the same Bible. We should all say the same prayers, we should all use those religious ideas that are common to all of us—meaning all of us Protestants.[11]

By 1900 and onward America had become increasingly urban as a result of high rates of immigration, which invariably led to a number of new social problems riling the concern of many of the nation's new wealthy elites, all of whom were well-connected to the political arena. This led many of these elites to begin to question the efficiency of local support of schools largely based on their growing concern with the failure of the schools to effectively "Americanize" students, especially those who were immigrants as well as those who were American but came from more "culturally deprived" areas (namely, black children and children of immigrants).

Essentially, the elites sought to secure that the values of the middle and upper class were the guiding forces of curriculum and schooling practices, leading them to use their financial resources to apply influence on the growing public sector of education, a trend that will become an increasingly important and, in many ways, deleterious component of the American public school system.

Their influence was successful, and for the first part of the 20th century, schools became intent on instilling the American ethic within all of its students by teaching only in English, requiring students to abandon their native cultural traditions in favor of their new American ones, and using textbooks that promoted American ideals as well as nonconflicting, romanticized accounts of the founding fathers (e.g., the widely popular McGuffey Readers).[12]

The perfusion of this sentiment to the very core of American policy is best demonstrated by Theodore Roosevelt who stated:

> We have room for but one language here [in America], and that is the English language. ... For we intend to see that the crucible turn our people out as Americans, of American nationality, and not as dwellers of a polygot boarding house.[13]

This sense of the need for nationalism increased with American involvement in World War I, during which the purpose of schooling to serve a nationalizing and Americanizing role was deepened, and it was to remain this way for several decades. According to Alfred Kazin, "officially the idea was to get us out of the barbarism of our immigrant background, but the [real] idea was to 'Americanize' us as they say, and it did."[14] Gilbert Gonzales recalls:

> Educational theory at the time [1960s] assumed that the persistence of the Spanish language constructed a barrier to educational achievement. And so the school system assumed that this was their burden to, in a way, "civilize" or "Americanize" the Mexican community. And the Mexican community recoiled at that.[15]

Along these same lines was the effort in the 1940s to require the recitation of the "Pledge of Allegiance," complete with its subsequently incorporated phrase "under God" at the beginning of the school day solely as a means of saturating the classroom, made up of largely children of immigrants, with the notion of "Americanism."[16] It followed that each classroom was to prominently don an American flag as well.

It appeared that the very intent of schooling in the early to mid-20th century was to instill and preserve white middle-class American values into the whole of society, preserving this value system as a standard which would be met, resulting in access to society, or failed to be met, resulting in marginalization and relegation to the fringes of society. This system preserved the status of those mostly white families who were already in the middle class, thus minimizing the chances of "backsliding" down the social ladder, while the capitalistic notion (which is largely mythical) of providing "free access" to resources in order to "create one's own share" was upheld.

As suggested by Katz, this represented the embodiment of Gramsci's ideas regarding coercive power by initiating "a direction imposed on social life by the dominant fundamental group."[17] David Brion Davis similarly suggests:

Ideological hegemony is not the product of conscious choice and seldom involves insincerity or deliberate deception. ... Ideology is a mode of consciousness, rooted in but not reducible to the needs of a social group. ... At issue, then, are not conscious intentions but the social functions of ideology; not individual motives but shifting patterns of thought and value which focused attention on new problems, which camouflaged others, and which defined new conceptions of social reality.[18]

Therefore, the emerging urbanizing and industrializing society, in its transformation from an agrarian one, was reasserting and reforming the system of elitism in its own, largely American brand, with the middle class gaining dominance over the public sector. The question became one of not only "civilizing" the poor and "culturally deprived," but also ameliorating the cultural (or multicultural) influence of the mass of immigrants by indoctrinating their children into the acceptable ways of American culture through the public school. According to Katz:

The impending rot of Anglo-American civilization could be averted through a concerted effort to shape the still pliable characters of [immigrants'] children into a native mold. This massive task of assimilation required weakening the connection between the immigrant child and its family, which in turn, required the capture of the child by an outpost of native culture. In short, the anxiety about cultural heterogeneity propelled the establishment of systems of public education; from the very beginning public schools became agents of cultural standardization.

NOTES

1. Ralph Waldo Emerson. (1841). Self Reliance. Retrieved from http://www.emersoncentral.com/selfreliance.htm.
2. WEB DuBois (1903) as cited by Tyack and Cuban, 69.
3. Tyack and Cuban, *Tinkering Toward Utopia*, 16.
4. Ravitch, *The Troubled Crusade*.
5. Ravitch, *The Troubled Crusade*, 86.
6. Katz, "The Origins of Public Education."
7. Ravitch, *The Troubled Crusade*, xii.
8. The Minnesota Chronicle and Register. Retrieved on September 28, 2015 from https://archive.org/stream/americansallimmi00unit/americansallimmi00unit_djvu.txt.
9. Horace Mann, as cited in Mondale, *School*, 29.
10. Ibid.
11. Ibid., 33.
12. Mondale, *School*.

13. Theodore Roosevelt, as cited by Mondale, *School*, 95.

14. Alfred Kazin, as cited by Mondale, *School,* 96–97.

15. Gilbert Gonzales as cited by Mondale, *School,* 152.

16. Kevin M. Kruse, *One Nation Under God: How Corporate America Invented Christian America* (New York: Basic Books, 2015).

17. Katz, "The Origins of Public Education."

18. Ibid.

Chapter 4

Schools of Thought

Systematizing the Study of Education

While the previous chapters made reference to various ideas regarding the purpose and role of public schools, there is a deeper narrative that must be engaged when exploring the specific types of educational reform and its respective reformers. Indeed, the two aspects are mutually dependent as the type of educational reform one calls for is necessarily an outgrowth of dissatisfaction with the current state of educational policy and practice, at least to some degree.

However, what is more deeply fascinating is the ostensibly clear notion that the arguments which ensue under the guise of public education tend to encompass, reflect, or at times even superimpose other fervent debates taking place in greater society. These larger issues include global economic competitiveness, cultural assimilation, literacy rates, career readiness, and unemployment, among panoply of others. This fervency, combined with the intense faith that many Americans place in the public school system as the site of righting social wrongs, leads to a seemingly endless continuance of educational reform on both small and large scales. According to Cuban and Tyack:

> From time to time, worries about society and schooling so accumulate that widespread educational reform ensues. In such periods the policy elites often take the lead in diagnosing problems and proposing educational solutions.[1]

The notion of the power of schooling is so engrained in the American social narrative that it shows up even in the rhetoric of presidents, such as Johnson's "Great Society" in which he proclaims, "The answer to all our national problems comes down to a single word: education."[2] While inspiring at face value, such intense expressions of faith often result in a trend of overpromising unrealistic ends on which schools cannot possibly deliver, thus creating the cycle of intensive efforts into public schooling followed by deep disappointment in its failure, further fueling the vicious circle of education reform.

When there is an accumulated social interest in particular problems, or such grave concern over greater society in general, education reform efforts seem to be the most likely conduit for such debates to take place as well as the vehicles by which politicians brandish their ideas for change and implement more socially and politically visible initiatives. The question then becomes: Under whose direction, expertise, and planning will should such reform take place, and based on what vision for America will it progress?

The notion that policy elites, who are most often either distant or entirely divorced from public educational processes at all, almost assuredly get the "final word" in the planning, designation, and implementation of curricular reform has been fodder for great unrest among many groups, including teachers, administrators, students, and parents, for several decades. These platforms not only encompass political and ideological competitions, but also economics, power dynamics, classism, racism, sexism, ageism, ableism, and a multitude of other important though potentially conflicting cultural and counter-cultural vantages and social processes. But what education reform actually is, not only in terms of political rhetoric but also in terms of real practice remains more elusive. As described by Tyack and Cuban, education reform can be seen

> neither as an ineluctable evolution—progressive or otherwise—nor as a set of fitful repetitions. Rather [it is] an interaction of long-term institutional trends, transitions in society, and policy talk.[3]

What ensues, then, in the name of education reform is a series of often ideologically and methodologically conflicting attempts to ameliorate social evils thought to have been propagated by past or current educational practices with the implementation of new, more enlightened approaches and guidelines. The outplay of these "new reforms" most often result in a confused, convoluted, unnavigable, and discursive system of schooling leaving old and new conflicting elements vying for dominance in an ill-equipped and ill-prepared system.

Adding to this complication is both the public and political desire for progress to be noticeable, if not be explicitly observable and measurable. These politically driven actions lead, all too often, to hasty conclusions, dissemination, and interpretation of unreliable and incomplete data collection and corresponding analysis, and the danger of using de-contextualized rhetoric for or against particular policies in order to fill the gaps between genuine information, ultimately serving largely political rather than truly socially significant means.

As Cuban and Tyack further describe, "Certain reforms may look successful when judged soon after adoption, but in fact they may turn out to be fireflies, flickering brightly but soon fading."[4] Beyond philosophy, however, an exploration of how education reform, that is the social reform thought to be achieved based on creating and continuously reforming the educational system, formed the basis of American public schooling from its very inception.

Perhaps the first "school of thought" established regarding the field of education was that of the *mental disciplinarians*,[5] the aforementioned "classical educationists" who regarded the mind as, quite literally, a muscle. Based largely on the philosophy of Plato, who believed that certain subjects were more powerful in developing the mind than others, the mental disciplinarians promulgated that the mind itself is strengthened using repetitious exercises based out of certain pivotal subjects such as Greek, Latin, mathematics, and literature.

Generally, because members of the mental disciplinarian paradigm, in many respects formalized by the National Education Association's creation of the Committee of Ten in 1892, were seen as largely academic and university-based, their ideas regarding curriculum for pre-college education was widely criticized as being based almost entirely on what would best prepare students for collegiate success. The committee, however, refuted such claims, suggesting that their only goal was to create a curriculum for "life," and that any parallels between their report and the college curriculum represented the congruence of the college curriculum to that of "life itself."[6]

Despite the general approbation of mental disciplinarian ideology and its seemingly direct influence on the early school curriculum, educational theoretical and curricular dominance during the first quarter of the 20th century was ultimately usurped by a group of educational and management scholars known as "social efficiency theorists"[7] or "administrative progressives."[8] The greater debate between the mental disciplinarians and the social efficiency theorists took shape virtually simultaneously with that of the growing, though far more esoteric discussion regarding the education of newly freed blacks in the south, exchanged mainly between Booker T. Washington, who supported vocational training (a la social efficiency) and W.E.B. DuBois, who supported classical education (a la mental disciplinarian).

However, the mental disciplinarians and social efficiency theorists framed their discussion within a more general social level and typically did not infuse their theories with issues of race. While the reason for this omission remains somewhat unclear, there are likely two general interpretations. One, that the public school system was either viewed as being intended for white students only (virtually all social efficiency theorists and mental disciplinarians were white elites, leading this to be the most likely explanation). Or, two, that for the theory itself, race was not an issue (a far more unlikely explanation).[9]

Perhaps the critical issue of the social efficiency theorists was prompted by Joseph Mayer Rice who, in 1892, conducted a "study" of classrooms in 36 cities around the United States. Rice's description of his observations encapsulated what would be considered prototypical mental disciplinarian curricular practice:

> Before the lesson began there was passed to each child a little flag, on which has been pasted various forms and colors, such as a square piece of green paper, a triangular piece of green paper, etc. When each child had been supplied, a signal was given by the teacher. Upon receiving the signal, the first child sprang up, gave the name of the geometrical form upon his flag, loudly and rapidly defined the form, mentioned the name of the color, and fell back into his seat to make way for the second child. ... This process was continued until each child in the class had recited. The rate of speed maintained during the recitation was so great that seventy children passed through the process of defining in a very few minutes."[10]

Further conclusions Rice made as a result of his studies were that many superintendents lacked any real expertise in pedagogy (a critique that can and is often still leveled today) and that there was no apparent definable connection between mental disciplinarian activities (such as "fact drilling" and "rule recitation") and student achievement. This ill-defined and nebulous concept will come to frame the goal of virtually all educational reform efforts over the last three centuries.

Rice's conclusion and prescription were clear: the largely useless drill and practice method of the mental disciplinarians can be countered by the development and proliferation of standards toward which all children must progress, and ultimately achieve. Regulation and evaluation of these standards were to be governed and monitored by school administrations using "a scientific system of pedagogical management [that] would demand fundamentally the measurement of results in the light of fixed standards."[11]

Following in line with rapid industrialization, Rice's ideas of systematically managing and monitoring educational endeavors were eagerly accepted, and the notion gradually transformed into the view that schools were best operated from the business-based perspective. As aforementioned, the scientific management strategies of Taylor regarding managing the efficiency of factories were suggested by Edward A. Ross to be equally as relevant to managing and improving the efficiency of schools. To Ross, the role of the school was clear and had been misinformed and mismanaged by the mental disciplinarians and the humanists: schools are not a tool of social change and societal development, but one of social control superior even to that of the church or the parent.

John Franklin Bobbitt, extending Taylor's and Ross's concept, began to propose that there can also be a scientific management of education, one that is deeply rooted in that of Taylor's factory-based theories. Based on this notion, schools became analogous to factories which turned out a product, a commodity of economic value which, in the case of a school, was a skilled worker able to contribute economically to his or her employer, family, as well as the greater economic well-being of his society. This perspective was a clear application of capitalistic viewpoints upon the role of schools, and was to remain a major element to the ensuing debate, ever-maintaining a principal, if not dominant presence, even in current discussions of schooling and education reform.

While the social efficiency theorists were gaining ground in the area of practice and curriculum, *humanism* was an inchoate though quickly developing frame of thought. In many ways humanism is linked to the mental disciplinarians through the formation of the Committee of Ten, as some of the original members would be more aptly defined as "humanists" rather than "mental disciplinarians." Thus, there is a deep connection between the development of both mental disciplinarian and humanist educational thought somewhat contemporaneously.

From the ongoing meetings of the Committee of Ten, what would become the humanist view of education was ultimately developed. That is, what would come to be called "humanism" was, ostensibly, a result of theoretical compromises between the separate schools of the "mental disciplinarians" and the nascent "humanists" largely as a response to the growing influence of social efficiency theorists on educational practice. Summarizing the humanist view, Charles Eliot, then president of Harvard, suggests:

> There has been too much reliance on the principle of authority, too little on the progressive and persistent appeal to reason ... [and] no amount of *memoriter* studied of languages or of the natural sciences and no attainments in arithmetic will protect a man or woman ... from succumbing to the first plausible delusion or sophism he or she may encounter.[12]

Clearly, much of the mental disciplinarian thought, such as that of memorization, was deftly replaced with a more socially relevant and functional focus. In many ways, this perspective of education was very much reflective of Jefferson and Adams who established that the purpose of education is not only social action but also liberation, such that citizens cannot fall victim to the deluded encounters to which Eliot refers. As such, humanists suggest that far more emphasis must be placed on thinking rather than simply accumulating knowledge, either in the mental disciplinarian form of facts and recitations or in the social efficiency form of vocational trades or work-based skills. These types of inculcations, humanists suggest, will have no effect on the development of one's sense of citizenship and civic duty.

Most importantly, however, and in direct contrast to the social efficiency theorists, humanists were staunchly opposed to distinguishing students based on who would or would not be expected to be attending college and directing their courses of either academic study or vocational training based on such a presumption. That is, the "school as sieve" function was seen as unjust to humanists, and could be interpreted as a means of perpetuating a hierarchy and, ultimately, a class-based social system not only maintained, but in some ways actually *created* by the school system.

The way in which humanists suggested that the theory be translated into curriculum was through the process of "electivism," or allowing students to choose one's own courses based on his or her intellectual or practical interests. By allowing self-choice, students would not be "tracked," or ultimately forced toward one particular predetermined future or another, but rather one that could be determined on their own. It is important, however, to not overly romanticize the humanist perspective. While acknowledging that though there was a general rejection of "tracking" and "sorting," the rejection was based primarily on the refutation of the notion that students known as "the army of incapables," whose burden served a central function to social efficiency theory, made up a significant portion of the population.

On that level, the humanists did not espouse the idea that justice was to be done for all, but rather that those for whom justice was not likely to be done represented an ineffectual proportion of the population and thus did need to be entered into the discussion at all. Hence, the humanistic proposition maintained the elitism of social efficiency theorists, albeit in a more covert manner.[13]

After the Committee of Ten report was released and the new school of "humanism" had been formally established, a group of opponents, who would come to be called *developmentalists*, would emerge as one of its main critics. One of the main proponents of developmentalism, G. Stanley Hall, reported the results of an 1893 study, which he claimed found that the contents of a child's mind could be identified through observation and will invariably change over time. As such, Hall suggested that these contents themselves, rather than a superimposed abstract theory of learning, should guide curriculum development.

Thus, developmentalists argued that not all elements of curriculum could (or should) be predetermined, and instead argued for a more fluid, flexible mode of practice. According to Hall, referring to school-aged children, "The pupil is in the age of spontaneous variation which at no period of life is so great. He does not want a standardized, overpeptonized mental diet. It palls on his appetite."[14]

Directly criticizing the Committee of Ten, Hall posits three main fallacies that were propagated by their report. First, he suggests that the Committee of Ten ultimately supports the notion of a standardized curriculum despite the caveat of "electivism." In this light, the developmentalists appeared to be in favor of tracking, as it was Hall's term of "army of incapables" to which Eliot responded despite Hall's allegiance to the developmentalists rather than the social efficiency theorists toward which Eliot leveled the criticism.

Second, all subjects were seen as having equal value if taught equally well, emphasizing that teaching and engaging the process of learning was the important component of schooling, not the subject itself. Third, and similarly to all aforementioned schools of educational theory, the developmentalists believed that the distinction between an educated class and a working class should be maintained, and the members of each class should be established by the school during the educational process.

In a direct response to Hall's criticisms, Eliot noted:

Thoughtful students of [Hall's theories] ... will refuse to believe that the American public intends to have its children sorted before their teens into clerks, watchmakers, lithographers, telegraph operators, masons, teamsters, farm laborers, and so forth, and treated differently in their schools according to these prophecies. ... Who are to make these prophecies?[15]

In a more formulated response to criticisms by the developmentalists as well as others, the National Education Association (NEA) reconvened a new group of scholars, unimaginatively named the Committee of Fifteen, with William Torrey Harris as its unofficial spokesman. In an attempt to directly address some of the critiques of the social efficiency theorists and the developmentalists upon the humanists, Harris maintained that humanism was the most appropriate frame for curriculum, but that it could be informed by standards, as per social efficiency, without sacrificing its humanistic integrity.

To better demonstrate his point Harris suggested the establishment of the "five windows of the soul" through which standards could be evaluated: grammar, literature and art, mathematics, geography, and history (though it is worthy to note that Harris was vocally suspicious of the natural sciences as a course of study and defended the centricity of the humanities in all legitimate educational endeavors). Equally as distrustful of the connection between industry and schools, the centerpiece of social efficiency, Harris believed that the role of schools was not to create workers and skilled laborers, but rather to pass on and preserve the heritage and virtue of Western culture.

As is often the case during critical periods of theoretical development, factions began to form within the humanist ranks that ultimately came to be seen as irreconcilably different, and therefore a push for a new, fundamentally distinct organization was needed. In response, a number of members of the NEA chartered a new association called the National Herbart Society, joined by those who believed deeply in the philosophy of Johann Friedrich Herbart, a German intellectual credited with legitimizing the field of pedagogy as an intellectual discipline.

Herbartian theory suggested that there was a deep interrelation between academic subjects and, therefore, such subjects could not be thoroughly studied and appreciated when approached in a fragmented fashion. This idea was a centerpiece of the ideas espoused by the mental disciplinarians, the social efficiency theorists, and even the new school humanists. Alternatively, Herbartians preferred the idea of the academic "concentration." That is, a particular subject can be set as the center-point for an intellectual exploration, but the goal of that exploration is to determine the many ways in which other subjects interrelate with the subject of concentration, such as how math connects to science as a result of social problems magnified by literature. This interconnection serves to minimize or, ideally, prevent the practice of regarding each subject as a separate entity.

Over time the National Herbart Society became so distinct from the new school humanists that they began to become known as *progressives*, embracing a rather imprecise description for virtually any idea that can be seen as nondominant and in opposition to the current state of affairs. In any case, the progressives became the dominant voice in educational theory and practice by the middle of the 1940s, in no small part due to the leviathan contributions of John Dewey, perhaps the most widely recognized, vocal, and influential member of what would become the Progressive movement.

The Progressives were clear in distinguishing themselves from all other schools of thought, including the humanists from which they developed, by declaring themselves as proponents of a "new education." This "new education" focused on flexible, child-centered, and democratic approaches, while the "old education," regardless of guiding philosophy, could be characterized as being rigid, subject-centered, and authoritarian.[16]

Maintaining the notions that schools were the center of social change, progressivism situated their pedagogy neither in terms of knowledge building nor in terms of preparation for society at a later time. Rather, progressives suggested that school was, indeed, society itself and that building a democratic school system was imperative in maintaining a democratic society outside of the schoolhouse. Essentially, the progressives rejected the traditional notions that schools' primary role was to improve intellectual functioning, minimized the importance of preserving national heritage through education, devalued book learning and focusing on traditional subjects, especially if they were tied to an inflexible daily schedule, eliminated the centricity of competing for external rewards of any type, and denigrated the dominance of the teacher in the educational process.

It is imperative, however, to maintain the context of the roots of progressive education within the larger progressive social movement, one that is not to be separated from that of the ever-present disagreement between capitalism and socialism. In this vein, the impetus for these ideas were largely anticapitalist and, in some ways, potentially viewed as socialist (though this, in itself, is debatable). This idea is epitomized in Dewey's declaration:

> [the] whole creed of complaisant [sic] capitalistic individualism and the right and duty of economic success commits [President Hoover] to the continuation of that hypocritical religion of "prosperity" which is, in my judgment, the greatest force that exists at present in maintaining the unrealities of our social tone and temper.[17]

Additional promotion of this view came from George S. Counts, who suggested that there was a deep connection between the socially unjust curriculum and the deterioration of the American society, in this case indicating the clear emergence of economic stratification and the establishment of the "selected few, whether by birth or by talent."[18] The result of this preoccupation with capitalism was a society that was not only undemocratic, but riddled with social injustice. Being that the school was to be seen as society itself, not as a preparatory process made up of exercises simulating citizenship to be used for later civic participation, Dewey and the Progressives viewed the school as the epicenter for true social change.

Based on this notion, the progressives believed that the immediate life of the child should be seen as the starting point for curriculum. This approach to curriculum allowed the child to discover his or her self-determined purposes in order to continuously develop an intellectual identity that is to contribute to the democratic functioning of the society.

For Dewey, democracy extends the notion of democratic governance in terms of representation and citizen participation, but rather is defined as a means of associated living comprised of individuals who participate in a way such that each has to refer one's own action to that of others, considering the action of others to give direction to his own. That is, self-interest is entirely ill-suited to a progressive philosophy, and ultimately democratic society, but rather what is good for the individual and the collective is to take precedence.

Enmeshed in this perspective is the notion that quality education cannot be a privilege afforded only to those who are wealthy enough to provide it privately or live in an affluent enough community whose taxes can support a reasonable public schooling operation, but rather must be made available to all individuals for the society in order to be truly democratic. As he states, "If democracy has a moral and ideal meaning, it is that a social return be demanded from all and that opportunity for development of distinctive capacities be afforded all."[19]

In direct opposition to progressivism, a school of thought known as "essentialism" began to emerge. Drawing on contrary tenets, essentialism posited that curriculum, in order to be effective, was to be systematic and sequential, applying carefully predesigned procedures and systems of study. Employing the ever-present context of rugged individualism (though somewhat weakened at the time due to a wider popular interest in socialism and collectivism) which held individuals to high standards of achievement, essentialists claimed that theories embracing the loosening of standards and promoting the importance of freedom, interest, and personal experience would lead to dire consequences despite their rhetorical appeal.

Such dire consequences were, implicitly, the value of the collective over the individual, and, potentially, embracing the socialistic principles from which the progressive perspective came. In many ways, essentialism can be regarded as re-branded social efficiency theory, in this case used to serve the purpose of directly contradicting progressivism, while traditional social efficiency theory was used to debunk mental disciplinarianism. Contemporary educational practices, especially those that mirror the Common Core State Standards and the ever-traditionalizing and manualized teaching practices, can most certainly be viewed as essentialist.

NOTES

1. Tyack & Cuban, *Tinkering Toward Utopic,* 41.
2. Lyndon B. Johnson as cited by Tyack and Cuban, *Tinkering Toward Utopia,* 2.
3. Tayck and Cuban, *Tinkering Toward Utopia,* 58.
4. Ibid., 7.
5. Kliebard, *The Struggle for the American Curriculum.*
6. Herbert M. Kliebard, "Three Currents of American Thought." 75–84. Retrieved on September 22, 2015 from http://www.google.com/url?sa=t&rct=j&q=&esrc=s&source=web&cd=3&ved=0CCYQFjACahUKEwji8r3U5YrIAhWIcD4KHYFSBXI&url=http%3A%2F%2Fgayleturner.net%2FThree%2520Currents.pdf&usg=AFQjCNFtfeaxXejFc2575BPqzVwZ6znvYg.
7. Ibid.
8. Tyack and Cuban, *Tinkering Toward Utopia.*
9. In any case, the issue of race is so deeply rooted in American public schooling that the following chapter will handle it as its own topic.
10. Joseph Mayer Rice, as cited by Kliebard, *The Struggle for the American Curriculum,* 18.
11. Ibid., 20.

12. Charles Eliot, as cited by Kliebard, *The Struggle for the American Curriculum,* 9.

13. Kliebard, *The Struggle for the American Curriculum.*

14. Ibid., 12.

15. Kliebard, *The Struggle for the American Curriculum,* 13.

16. Kliebard, *The Struggle for the American Curriculum.*

17. John Dewey, as cited by Kliebard, *The Struggle for the American Curriculum,* 151.

18. George S. Counts, as cited by Kliebard, *The Struggle for the American Curriculum,* 154.

19. John Dewey, *Democracy and Education* (New York: Free Press, 1916/1997), 122.

Chapter 5

The Flat Free World

Global Competitiveness and Equal Educational Opportunity

The battle for ownership of curriculum and dominance in dictating the purpose of American schooling does not end with the essentialists, but rather continues in what appears to be a vicious circle rife with both social and historical amnesia and conflicting claims to proprietary rights. The way in which various schools of thought translate their ideas into practice is by winning the approval of the policy elites; those who, despite knowing little, if anything about education have the greatest access to and power over the political and legislative players that regulate it. The means by which such initiatives come about and, equally as important, the means by which they are ultimately eliminated or replaced are often where the true contentiousness lies.

In American education reform there appears to be some general trends that act as catalysts for such change, as well as respective legislation or policy implementation through which such philosophical changes are compelled in practice. Thus, it is argued that the following four catalysts can be traced throughout the history of American public education and have resulted in multiple variations of educational reform: (1) the need for global competitiveness in order to regain and/or maintain American economic supremacy; (2) educational accessibility for "all" children across racial, ethnic, linguistic, and economic boundaries; (3) support for centralization or decentralization of the public school system; and (4) interest and power of private sector and corporate entities to enhance financial and political control over public domains.

Indeed, while such catalysts are separated for analysis, it is quite clear that any combination, if not all, can be at work simultaneously, and that one, namely corporate interest, bears far more influence than the others in contemporary public educational practice. The tendency to separate such issues comes more often as a result of political categorization and agenda itemization rather than genuine distinctions between the natures of issues.

THE NEED TO REGAIN OR MAINTAIN GLOBAL COMPETITIVENESS (OR SUPREMACY)

Many calls for educational change that come as a plea to either strive to regain the spirit and society of some likely over-romanticized past era or to move beyond an immoral present toward a more just future have been recapitulated multiple times throughout history. In either case, the advocates of each side yearn for a different America: either one that has been lost or one that has yet to be found. As suggested by Ravitch:

> Educational institutions became focal points for large areas of consensus ... [as well as] magnets for dissension, attracting all those who wanted to change the social order, preserve threatened traditions, challenge historic wrongs, or make sure that the next generation was not tainted by the errors of their predecessors.[1]

Elements of concern with global competitiveness can be traced across centuries as well. Consider the following statements by Theodore Search, then president of the National Association of Manufacturers (1898), and John Akers, former chairman of IBM (1991), identified by Cuban.[2] Search contends:

> There is hardly any work we can do or any expenditures we can make that will yield so large a return to our industries as would come from the establishment of educational institutions which would give us skilled hands and trained minds for the conduct of our [sic] industries and our commerce.[3]

Nearly a century later, Akers indicates a similar frame of thought and a provoking consideration of whether schools have simply failed, or whether the focus on the purpose of school has simply remained inadequate:

> Education isn't just a social concern, it's a major economic issue. If our students can't compete today, how will our companies compete tomorrow? In an age when a knowledgeable workforce is a nation's most important resource, American students rank last internationally in calculus and next to last in algebra.[4]

Therefore, while there has ever been, and likely ever will be, a push-pull dynamic to education reform, the issues between generations can be a difficult one to rectify. Generational divides between propitious pasts and ideal futures are analytically precarious, likely because such analysis and interpretation are dependent on generations to go through school and grow old enough to reflect in order to have any significance. Through the 1940s, Gallup polls consistently reported that upward of 85 percent of respondents indicated that they believed the current youth were getting a better education than they did,[5] though this coincides with more formal schooling approaches and a bettering economy after the Depression was weathered, unmistakably resulting in a higher nationalistic morale as well as a general sense of optimism.

This morale was to be dealt a distinct blow when, in 1957, Russia "won" the "Space Race" with its successful launching and resulting orbit of Sputnik. At once the global economic and intellectual dominance of "Americans" was challenged, resulting in an eruption of pessimism in the public educational system which was now seen, for the first time, as "failing," with the greater society needing no more proof than its defeat in space travel against its sworn enemy, ever thought to be a sure victory. This social disaster prompted much attention in both the public and private sectors, resulting in numerous efforts to improve American schools in the area of science and technology including financial grants made by both the Ford Foundation and Carnegie Foundation, a situation analogous to the current focus on Science, Technology, Engineering, and Math, or STEM areas.

This sentiment lasted for a number of decades, and precipitated critically once again in 1983 with the release of the most ominous and damning of official invectives against public education, *Nation at Risk*. This resultantly ineluctable narrative was the culminating report of the National Commission on Excellence in Education, initiated by then Secretary of Education T.H. Bell in response to his concern about "the widespread public perception that something is seriously remiss in [America's] educational system."[6] One specific concern cited by the Committee was the issue of declining quality of education between generations, as it states:

> What was unimaginable a generation ago has begun to occur—others are matching and surpassing our educational attainments. … If an unfriendly foreign power had attempted to impose on America the mediocre educational performance that exists today, we might well have viewed it as an act of war.[7]

Using a common strategy of hyperbole in reports employing nationalistic rhetoric, the Commission suggested that America's education system had not simply declined, but had declined so severely that it could be seen as an aggressive act analogous to that of domestic terrorism. Such rhetoric also reinforces the notion of America's position in global competitiveness, which the Commission deems as being threatened, if not eliminated. As the report states:

> [America's] once unchallenged preeminence in commerce, industry, science, and technological innovation is being overtaken by competitors throughout the world. … Japanese make automobiles more efficiently. … South Koreans recently built the world's most efficient steel mill. … American machine tools, once the pride of the world, are being displaced by German products.[8]

How then are these matters of nationalistic concern connected directly to the education system? The Commission makes it quite clear in their assessment section of the report, which they entitle "Indicators of the Risk," citing a number of matters demonstrating this threat including[9]:

- International comparisons of student achievement, completed a decade before, reveal that on 19 academic tests American students were never first or second and, in comparison with other industrialized nations, were ranked last seven times.
- Average achievement of high school students on most standardized tests is now lower than 26 years prior when Sputnik was launched.
- The College Board's Scholastic Aptitude Test (SAT) demonstrated a virtually unbroken decline from 1963 to 1980. Average verbal scores fell over 50 points and average mathematics scores dropped nearly 40 points.
- Business and military leaders complain that they are required to spend millions of dollars on costly remedial education and training programs in such basic skills as reading, writing, spelling, and computation.

While representing only a sample of the indicators postulated in the report, the message is quite clear: American students were falling horrifyingly far behind other nations, and the subpar educational system was to blame. The historical context was also clear: if America could not win the Space Race 26 years earlier when schools were markedly better, there is no possibility of regaining supremacy if the schools are now so declined. As a final blow, the report indicated that the eroding quality of schools is not just an indication of waning intelligence or a matter of economic prosperity, but one of national security, as our "youngsters" are so in need of remediation that they are incapable of grasping the information necessary to be a trained member of the "modern military."

The veracity of this rhetoric, however, is entirely dependent on the capitalistic centricity of America. That is not to say that it is only capitalistic economies that are focused on money, but rather that it is patently capitalistic societies that remain indefatigably defensive of their economic dominance, and can therefore successfully use rhetoric of global economic dominance as a rallying cry to action. As Postman suggests:

> America is not so much a country as it is an economy [and] ... the vitality of the nation's economy rests on high standards of achievement and rigorous discipline in school ... those who believe in it are inclined to compare American schoolchildren to those of children from other countries. The idea is to show that the Americans do not do as well in certain key subjects, thus accounting for failures in American productivity. There are several problems with this logic,

among the difficulties in comparing groups that differ greatly in their traditions, language, values, and general orientation to the world.[10]

Indeed, this sentiment remains dominant in the rhetoric of the Obama administration (2008–2016). In a comment relating to the Department of Education's *Race to the Top* initiative, Obama declares:

> America will not succeed in the 21st century unless we do a far better job of educating our sons and daughters. ... And the race starts today. I am issuing a challenge to our nation's governors and school boards, principals and teachers, businesses and non-profits, parents and students: if you set and enforce rigorous and challenging standards and assessments; if you put outstanding teachers at the front of the classroom; if you turn around failing schools—your state can win a Race to the Top grant that will not only help students outcompete workers around the world, but let them fulfill their God-given potential.[11]

EDUCATIONAL ACCESSIBILITY FOR ALL CHILDREN THROUGH STANDARDS AND ACHIEVEMENT

Few truly socially aware members of American society could disagree with the notion that race and racism has played, and continues to play, a fundamental role in systemic institutions. While a deeper analysis of race will be dealt with in great detail later, it is important to establish important rhetoric instituted by very deliberate legislative language. This is especially important in light of its vast disjoint with actual practice, funding efforts, and legitimate investment, essentially only paying "lip service" to correcting systemic issues based on race.

As early as the 1950s, as de jure segregation was the normative practice in the South and de facto segregation was widespread in the North, there began a critical interest in the quality of education that black children were receiving, especially as it compared to the quality of education provided to their white counterparts. According to Clark:

> These [black] children, by and large, do not learn because they are not being taught effectively and they are not being taught because those who are charged with the responsibility do not believe they can learn, and do not act toward them in ways which help them learn.[12]

This characterization is strikingly similar to the rhetoric put forth by George W. Bush supporting No Child Left Behind regarding the "soft bigotry of low expectations."[13] Clark connected the critical social opinion of black Americans with the perniciously abject state of education in their communities.

Essentially, the notion that culturally deprived people created their own realities was hard at work in justifying the blame-basis for deep-seated social problems.

The Elementary and Secondary Education Act of 1965 (ESEA), the root legislation of the controversial *No Child Left Behind Act* of 2001, is a prudent starting point for demonstrating the legislative outcomes of this catalyst for educational reform, as it was the first attempt for educational legislation sanctioned by the federal government. The main goal of the Act was "to strengthen and improve educational quality and educational opportunities in the Nation's elementary and secondary schools." According to the Act:

> In recognition of the special educational needs of children of low-income families and the impact that concentrations of low income families have on the ability of local educational agencies to support adequate educational programs, the Congress hereby declares it to be the policy of the United States to provide financial assistance (as set forth in this title) to local educational agencies serving areas with concentrations of children from low-income families to expand and improve their educational programs by various means (including preschool programs) which contribute particularly to meeting the special educational needs of educationally deprived children.[14]

While cloaked within the context of "low-income families," echoing the common claim made by emerging areas of social science such as sociology that poverty, not race, was the main culprit of inequality, it is virtually inarguable that the thrust of this legislative action was to increase financial assistance to predominantly black (and, eventually Hispanic) neighborhoods that were plagued by low quality schools. Though from one perspective this newfound faith in public education should, indeed, be celebrated, there came to appear many more reasons by which these intense new charges against poverty as the culprit for "low achievement" should be met with suspicion, if not outright rejection, especially given the reality of the actual investment in proportion to the expectations made of the schools.

That is, the underlying notion was that, with money alone, schools should and would be able to fix all of the underlying social problems plaguing these communities despite the systemic impoverishment and marginalization of black communities, especially since World War II. According to James B. Conant:

> When one considered the total situation that has been developing in the Negro city slums since World War II, one has reason to worry about the future. The building up of a mass of unemployed and frustrated Negro youth in congested areas of a city is a social phenomenon that may be compared to the piling up of inflammable material in an empty building in a city block. Potentialities for trouble—indeed possibilities of disaster—are surely there.[15]

Therefore, it is likely that the political expectations of the school were less focused on true belief in its power, rather than its availability as a much needed scapegoat toward which unreasonably high expectations were input despite unreasonably low support, financial, social, or otherwise. Additionally, the role these financial efforts would play in the political posturing that was allowed by such infusion of federal monies cloaked as attention to matters of civil rights and race relations was significant. Ultimately, public schools began to be seen as simultaneously the cause and the solution to all of America's social ills. The most likely culprits of this dire situation were the low standards and subpar educational achievements plaguing the schools of socioeconomically challenged students.

This sentiment is resonant with the almost fundamental notion of a capitalistic society that poverty, rather than being a social issue to be contextualized within a dysfunctional system of government and an inherently unjust system of wealth distribution, is a sign of personal, or even cultural, defect, which can only be addressed and ameliorated through formal, institutional attention to the individual as designed and dictated by the hegemonic culture. Essentially, this system would result in yet another form of welfare practices designed to maintain cultural blame for its failure as well as laud political effort for its implementation.

This notion of increased standards, educational achievement, and its close ties to the receipt of funds has a deep and rich history in American public school legislation, beginning with the ESEA. As indicated in Section 205, Part 5 of ESEA:

> ...effective procedures, including provision for appropriate objective measurements of educational achievement, will be adopted for evaluating at least annually the effectiveness of the programs in meeting the special educational needs of educationally deprived children.

This sentiment of educational access is closely echoed in *Nation at Risk* some twenty years later, which states:

> All, regardless of race or class or economic status, are entitled to a fair chance and to the tools for developing their individual powers of mind and spirit to the utmost. This promise means that all children by virtue of their own efforts, competently guided, can hope to attain the mature and informed judgment needed to secure gainful employment, and to manage their own lives, thereby serving not only their own interest but also the progress of society itself.[16]

The notion of educational equity as the means of attaining economic contributive capability was to prove a resonant theme in all of the proceeding legislative acts handling education. However, the efforts toward actually attaining and maintaining "equity" in itself received far less attention than that of investing in demonstrating student achievement. That is, though the sentiment carried the rhetoric of equity for "educationally deprived children," the measure, or the true indicator of whether equity was being attained was evaluated only in terms of educational achievement. Though vastly insufficient, achievement was and is invariably defined in terms of standardized testing results; that is, the ends should be the focus of the monetary investment rather than the means and the process of the education itself.

This theme of higher standards and higher achievement proved recalcitrant in what was to become the next major political campaign for public education which came to fruition under the administration of President George H.W. Bush. In a massive call to action, President Bush organized a summit in Charlottesville, held at the University of Virginia, which was open to the governors of all 50 states (49 out of the 50 governors were in attendance, with the exception of Rudy Perpich, a Democrat from Minnesota).[17] At this summit Bush fervently urged the governors to take a more distinct interest in K-12 education, especially in the area of increasing academic standards.

Additionally, Bush called for a "corporate style" approach to implementing such standards and monitoring progress toward achievement—one based in accountability, especially regarding those responsible for delivering them. This effort culminated in an effort called "America 2000," which was a voluntary program by which states would adopt national standards and testing procedures as an act of good faith toward improving educational outcomes for American children. This effort, however, was never passed by Congress, and therefore remained the work-product of a summit, rather than a viable piece of educational legislation.

The spirit of the Charlottesville summit remained strongly intact during the administration of President Bill Clinton who led a virtually identical initiative entitled "Goals 2000," which declared[18]:

1. By the year 2000, all children will start school ready to learn.
2. By the year 2000, the high school graduation rate will increase to at least 90 percent.
3. By the year 2000, American students will leave grades 4, 8, and 12 having demonstrated competency in challenging subject matter, including English, mathematics, science, history, and geography, and every school in America will ensure that all students learn to use their minds well, so they may be prepared for responsible citizenship, further learning, and productive employment in our modern economy.
4. By the year 2000, U.S. students will be first in the world in mathematics and science achievement.

5. By the year 2000, every adult American will be literate and will possess the skills necessary to compete in global economy and exercise the rights and responsibilities of leadership.
6. By the year 2000, every school in American will be free of drugs and violence and will offer a disciplined learning environment conducive to learning.

While "Goals 2000" was little more than a political initiative, it ultimately led directly to the reauthorization of the ESEA under the name "Improving America's Schools Act" (IASA) in 1994. This Act upheld many of the tenets put forth in the original ESEA, but made significant adjustments to the ways in which education was funded by the federal government, which was unprecedentedly increased, especially those funds appropriated to Title I, which addressed the needs of schools in challenged socioeconomic areas.

Endemic in the redesigning of Title I was the notion that states were preoccupied with meeting regulatory mandates of the Title, allowing for little effort to be placed on actually increasing attainment of educational achievement based on higher standards. Under IASA, schools were directed to refocus their attention to ensuring that children in high poverty schools are expected to achieve the same high standards that the state expects of all other schools, with Title I funds to be used in order to extend the school day before and after school programs as well as summer programs, as well as other efforts. Finally, IASA reframed the system of accountability for schools in terms of educational achievement by implementing a system of assistance, rewards, and sanctions based directly on outcomes of student achievement.

While IASA reframed the concepts of many aspects of the federal legislation used to regulate schooling and place standards upon state governments, little actual oversight and compliance appeared to be present until the administration of the proceeding president, George W. Bush reauthorized the legislation. The catalytic and largely ceremonious reauthorization and renaming of the Elementary and Secondary Education Act to the now ubiquitous, if not notorious "No Child Left Behind" Act of 2001(NCLB) echoes the same sentiments of the achievement gap between "advantaged" and "disadvantaged" children. According to Title I, Section 1001 a main priority of the law is in the area of

> meeting the educational needs of low-achieving children in our Nation's highest-poverty schools, limited English proficient children, migratory children, children with disabilities, Indian children, neglected or delinquent children, and young children in need of reading assistance … [and] closing the achievement gap between high- and low-performing children, especially the achievement gaps between minority and nonminority students, and between disadvantaged children and their more advantaged peers.[19]

Carrying the notion of the disparity between those who are disadvantaged and those who are not, NCLB was precedent setting not based on the putative effort toward the disadvantaged, but by tying the context of narrowing the achievement gap directly with rigorous standards, which were to become the sole purpose of the educational reform effort under Obama's administration in the 2010s. As stated in Section 1001(1) of NCLB:

Ensuring high quality academic assessments, accountability systems, teacher preparation and training, curriculum, and instructional materials are aligned with challenging State academic standards so that students, teachers, parents, and administrators can measure progress against common expectations for student academic achievement.

NCLB also made accountability for schools far more stringent by using much the same system as that which was laid out in the IASA, Section 1001(4) and 1001(6):

Holding schools, local educational agencies, and States accountable for improving the academic achievement of all students, and identifying and turning around low-performing schools that have failed to provide high-quality education to their students, while providing alternatives to students in such schools to enable the students to receive a high quality education (4) ... [and] improving and strengthening accountability, teaching, and learning by using State assessment systems designed to ensure that students are meeting challenging State academic achievement and content standards and increasing achievement overall, but especially for the disadvantaged.

These carefully chosen words make clear that the federal government is not "imposing" particular standards upon states, but rather setting centralized "guidelines" by which states are mandated to abide in the way that their governments, education departments, and local educational agencies decree. This language is careful not to breach the distinction between local, state, and federal control over the specific educational policies, especially under a staunchly conservative Republican administration. As such, NCLB issues specific decrees by which state governments must design educational policy with increased accountability mechanisms. According to Section 1111(C and D):

The State shall have such academic standards for all public elementary schools and secondary school children, including [disadvantaged children] in subjects determined by the State, but including at least mathematics, reading or language arts, and ... science, which shall include the same knowledge, skills, and levels of achievement expected of all children ... [States shall adopt] challenging academic content standards in academic subjects that specify what children are expected to know and be able to do, contain coherent and rigorous content, and encourage the teaching of advanced skills; and challenging student academic achievement standards that are aligned with the State's academic content standards, describe two levels of high achievement (proficient and advanced) that determine how well children are mastering the material in the State academic content standards; and describe a third level of achievement (basic) to provide complete information about the progress of the lower-achieving children toward mastering the proficient and advanced levels of achievement.

The notion of challenging academic standards and equitable expectations between challenged schools and affluent schools are made clear in America's history of educational legislation, setting an unmistakable tone that the "outcome" far exceeds the "means" in terms of importance. That is, it is of little importance to governments *how* such achievements are begotten, but rather that they *are* begotten. This major hole in policy has allowed for the introduction of myriad efforts by many organizations, private, corporate, and public, to develop and market "proven" ways to attain academic achievement.

NOTES

1. Ravitch, *The Troubled Crusade,* xii.
2. Larry Cuban, as cited by Mondale, *School,* 173.
3. Theodore Search, 1898, as cited in Patton and Mondale, *School,* 173.
4. Patton and Mondale, *School.*
5. Kliebard, *The Struggle for the American Curriculum.*
6. *Nation at Risk,* http://www2.ed.gov/pubs/NatAtRisk/risk.html.
7. Ibid.
8. Ibid.
9. Ibid.
10. Postman, *End of Education,* 28–29.
11. Barack Obama, July 24, 2009. www.whitehouse.gov/the-press-office/fact-sheet-race-top).
12. Clark, as cited by Ravitch, *The Troubled Crusade,* 58.
13. http://www.washingtonpost.com/wp-srv/onpolitics/elections/bushtext071000.htm.
14. Elementary and Secondary Education Act of 1965, http://www.gpo.gov/fdsys/pkg/STATUTE-79/pdf/STATUTE-79-Pg27.pdf.
15. James B. Conant, as cited by Ravitch, *The Troubled Crusade,* 150.
16. *Nation at Risk,* http://www2.ed.gov/pubs/NatAtRisk/risk.html.
17. Alyson Klein, "Historic Summit Fueled Push for K-12 Standards" *Education Week,* September 23, 2014. Retrieved from http://www.edweek.org/ew/articles/2014/09/24/05summit.h34.html on September 16, 2015.

18. Ibid.

19. Elementary and Secondary Education Act, retrieved from http://www2.ed.gov/policy/elsec/leg/esea02/pg1.html.

Chapter 6

Our Kids, Our Rules

Centralizing or Decentralizing America's Schools

Inherent in the argument about the purpose of public schooling is a stirring debate regarding the locus of control over public schooling. While there are, indeed, degrees of supervisory roles and control that differ between states, districts, and even individual schools within districts, this element of education reform appears to almost always vacillate between two general principles. One is total centralization, or near-total control by a governmental agency such as state departments of education or, in some contemporary ways, an increasing regulatory function of the federal government. The other is decentralization, or near-total control by local agencies such as district-based boards of education, administrations, and teachers.

While during the beginning phases of the development of the public schooling system in the United States schools were controlled and funded almost entirely by local entities with very little oversight or regulation, once aid was provided by the federal government and legislation, namely through Elementary and Secondary Education Act (ESEA) in 1965, a tenuous and precarious boundary was created between the level of control that the federal government, and in some cases state government, was to have in educational oversight beyond the provision of funding—an issue that is of utmost importance in the contemporary context of education.

Though elements of the centralization versus decentralization controversy were clear as early as 1919, with Charles Judd of the University of Chicago calling for the abolition of local school boards in favor of centralized boards, the first indication of this debate at the federal level became evident in the early 1970s under the Nixon administration, whose conservative policies generally reflected efforts toward a smaller, decentralized federal government, with the area of education to be no different. The first initiative under Nixon's decentralization effort was called the Experimental Schools Program (ESP), a

59

clear precursor for the 21st century's Race to the Top (RTT) initiative, though with a number of apparent differences.

While many of the details of the plan remained unclear even at the time of implementation, essentially schools were encouraged to make comprehensive "non-traditionalizing" efforts in educational areas including curriculum development, staff development, community involvement, and organization around a central theme that reflected and highlighted the change to be made (e.g., enhancing the skills of future workers).

Mainly as an attempt to correct what was perceived as the overpromising and extravagant agenda of Johnson's Great Society, the ESP gave way to a number of educational experiments. The open education movement attempted to change the methods and the goals of schooling overall especially in the refocusing of the role of the teacher, offering totally child-driven curriculum, and the absence of tests or formalized assessment of any kind. The free school movement sought to create a loose network of child-centered schools valuing character development over academic learning. The alternative school movement sought to apply elements of the "free school" into public schools. Finally, the "deschooling" movement proffered the radical idea that out-of-school activities had equal, if not superior, educational value and schools were, essentially, ineffectual and unnecessary.[1]

Following Johnson's presidency, the election of a conservative Republican administration tamed federal influence in education a bit, though spending remained. Nixon's efforts intentionally left decision making to the states. Reagan's administration sought a large-scale reduction in both the size of government as well as its involvement in traditionally state-based entities such as education. George H.W. Bush's America 2000, while calling for a move toward national standards, maintained the same distinction between federal and state powers by making his program strictly voluntary to the states, and even the passage of IASA under Clinton and NCLB under George W. Bush, despite increases in spending and monetary provision by the federal government, maintained that separation between federal and state control.

It was not until the Obama administration, under the tutelage of Arne Duncan, Obama's Secretary of Education for the majority of both presidential terms, that the direct influence of the federal government in educational policy became a distinct concern in the area of separation of powers. Initially proposed as a bill and inserted into the then current version of the ESEA as Section 6301 Part C, *Race to the Top* was an appendage of the *American Reinvestment and Recovery Act*, an effort by the staunchly liberal Obama administration to re-infuse monies into a number of public entities in light of troubled economic times, typified by a deep recession. RTT represented a $4.5 billion investment into the American public school system. According to the legislative text, the purposes of RTT were to provide incentives for States and local educational agencies to implement comprehensive reforms and innovative strategies that are designed to lead to—significant improvements in outcomes for all students, including improvements in student achievement, high school graduation rates, college enrollment rates and rates of college persistence; and significant reductions in achievement gaps among subgroups of students and encourage broad identification, adoption, use, dissemination, replication, and expansion of effective State and local policies and practices that lead to significant improvement in outcomes for all students, and the elimination of those policies and practices that are not effective at improvement student outcomes.[2]

The language employed in this section is all too familiar, resonant of the reduction of achievement gaps, increased standards, student achievement and outcomes, and comprehensive reforms at the state level. What made RTT most significant, however, was its presentation as a competitive grant. That is, these were not monies that were guaranteed to be provided to *all* states to support their educational reform efforts. Rather, these monies were to be made available to some states, in different denominations, based on competitive applications addressing specific areas of concern:

Each state and local educational agency receiving a grant under this part shall establish performance measures and targets, approved by the Secretary, for the programs and activities carried out under this part. These measures shall, at minimum, track the State's or agency's progress in—implementing its plan; and improving outcomes for all subgroups ... by—increasing student achievement; decreasing achievement gaps; increasing high school graduation; increasing college enrollment and persistence rates; improving the effectiveness of teachers and school leaders, increasing the retention of effective teachers and school leaders, and promoting equity in the distribution of effective teachers and school leaders to ensure that low-income and minority children are not—taught by ineffective teachers at higher rates than other children; and enrolled in schools led by ineffective leaders at higher rates than other children; increasing kindergarten readiness; and making progress on any other measures identified by the Secretary.[3]

The purported idea behind this grant, and its competitive nature, was to increase the "teeth" that past educational reforms did not have. That is, when all states were virtually guaranteed to receive some level of funding, minimal effort toward accountability was made as the monies were only loosely tied to demonstrating such accountability. However, for RTT, the monies available were not only significant in sum, but also significant in its limited availability. This competitive nature was one of the first critiques leveled toward the program, with the main thrust of the disagreement being that the federal government was overstepping its authority by "dangling carrots" in front of states, essentially compelling compliance to what was seen as more strict federal regulations and a potential breach of federal power over the states. According to Obama:

> This is one of the largest investments in education reform in American history. And rather than divvying it up and handing it out, we are letting states and school districts compete for it. That's how we can incentivize excellence and spur reform and launch a race to the top in America's public schools.[4]

While many of these critiques may likely have been fueled by political and ideological fervor, as the Obama administration drew much criticism on many issues due to its perceived radical use of legislative loopholes and powerful plays of politics and alliances, especially by Republicans, the genuine critics were sensing something that was even more legitimately disturbing. That is, a complex and clandestine interplay between the corporate elites and the governmental structure was to have an unprecedented and seemingly indelible effect on the boundaries between the private and public sectors. These new types of relationships earnestly tested, and in some cases straddled, the separation between federal and state powers in matters of education as never before.

One distinctly confounding aspect to the discussion of governmental regulation and influential latitude comes in the form of financial contribution and responsibility. While it is clear that most of the operating budgets for schools and school districts come from local taxes and state provided budgetary contributions, there has been, since at least the 1960s, significant involvement of federal government spending in schools as well. These tripartite sources of monetary assistance muddy the waters of leadership and complicate the roles of each party when it comes to budgetary decision making. As Edley suggests:

> Closely tied to the problem of school finance is the question of education governance. To whom do the people delegate responsibility for our schools, and with what consequences for legal and political accountability when we are dissatisfied the results? School finance inequalities illuminate both the vertical and horizontal dimensions of this question.[5]

It is by this very logic that RTT managed to pit states against one another to vie for large sums of money, while continuing to place responsibility for the success of such proposed programs directly on teachers and administrators, therefore eliminating the responsibility from the federal government in all matters but those that are financial. However, as the processes that lay just behind the public workings of RTT unfold, that close tie between governmental mandates and private corporate interests and influence becomes dishearteningly clear, and a veritable hostile takeover of public schools by private entities was successfully fulfilled through a "carrot" offered on behalf of the federal government.

Because America is a radically capitalistic country, so much so that it has even been suggested that "Americanism" is not a culture, but rather an economic way of life,[6] it stands to reason that business leaders are quite often seen as the paragon of success. This connection, while not only powerful in terms of global competitiveness, becomes exceedingly powerful when yoked with the purpose of education. That is, if one is to be successful in America, and the paramount of the American brand of success is wealth and prominence in business, then schools should be reflective of not only a business mentality and design, but be influenced and controlled directly by such businesses and its leaders.

Indeed, if participation in business and wealth appreciation is the goal for American children, then those who have attained it are apt to be the most effective contributors to such a design. This frame of thought exemplifies two common themes in American elitism and corporatism: (1) that there is, and should be, a general lack of trust in the capability of the greater American public; and (2) that the rich and elite are to be seen as the guardians and protectors of the American public's inevitable incompetence and failure.

Elements of this mentality have been present since the beginning of the 20th century when the aforementioned Charles Judd of the University of Chicago argued that local school boards should be replaced with boards made up of "experts" who are certified by the state, thus facilitating a truly top-down model. Such experts would be drawn from a pool of business and professional elites who would be responsible for transforming the "politics" of schooling to a more organized system of functioning, similar to that of a successful business. In this light, Judd set forth the *Manual of Educational Legislation* in 1919, which mapped the process of changing schools to a "business model." This idea was so well-received that by 1925 nearly 40,000 schools across 34 states had adopted its tenets with orthodoxy.[7]

Around the same time employees of the US Bureau of Education (the predecessor to the Department of Education) had their salaries subsidized by the John D. Rockefeller General Education Board, further establishing deep ties between governmental efforts and "charitable" corporate organizations that is likely comparable to the contemporary notion of "venture philanthropy" and its common connection with charter schools. Also aforementioned, the efforts by Albert Lynd propagated the continuation of corporate interest through the 1950s. In the 1960s and 1970s large-scale businesses, including defense contractors, were "hired" by the government to transform "at risk" schools by establishing private learning centers, such as the well-known Texarkana project, which were not dissimilar from current-day charter schools.

Private corporate interest and leadership in public education was not limited to local interests only, however, as is made clear by George H.W. Bush's establishment of the New American Schools Development Corporation (NASDC), created in direct service to the newly established America 2000 campaign. NASDC, which was comprised primarily of chief executive officers of private companies, was charged to quite literally *invent* the best schools in the world. In fact, the business model adopted by the NASDC was quite evident in its goals: (1) apply a "no-nonsense business approach"; (2) implement wholesale redesign of "break the mold" schools to be supported by the private venture; and (3) use a venture capitalist model of investment.

There is little doubt that these tenets, along with permissive legislative acts enhancing the legal influence of the private sector in public education, are what led to the considerable increase in charter schools in the late 20th century through the current time. This frame of thought persists in the current discourse over the Common Core State Standards (CCSS), and whether it is truly an effort toward educational reform or a product of corporate interests in public education made allowable by its lobby's influence on legislation.

While the rhetoric emphatically maintains that the CCSS were devised and proffered by a consortium of education professionals facilitated by the National Governor's Association and the Council of Chief State School Officers (CCSSO), the effort was influenced almost entirely by politically connected and corporate backed organizations, albeit those whose financial focuses were matters of education, including Achieve, Inc., the Bill and Melinda Gates Foundation, and the College Board, calling the purity of such efforts being in the spirit of educational reform as opposed to corporate interest into clear question. One such sentiment was expressed by Professor Jay P. Greene, Distinguished Professor at the University of Arkansas, who stated:

> There is no evidence that the Common Core standards are rigorous or will help produce better results. The only evidence in support of Common Core consists of projects funded directly or indirectly by the Gates Foundation in which panels of selected experts are asked to offer their opinion of the Common Core standards. Not surprisingly, panels organized by the backers of the Common Core believe that Common Core is good. This is not research; this is just advocates of the Common Core re-stating their support. The few independent evaluations of Common Core that exist suggest that its standards are mediocre and represent little change from what most states already have.[8]

As Greene's testimony indicates, despite the clear language of evidence basis stipulated in virtually all educational legislation including the supplementary materials of the CCSS, the sanctioned standards offered by the Common Core initiative lacks, at its very basis, any evidentiary support at all and, in fact, contraindications are increasingly being reported.[9,10] This concern represents only a part of the mounting narrative that is serving to not only invalidate the educational value of the Common Core, but expose the truth that the Common Core and its companion testing initiatives serve only to benefit corporate interests who are now permissibly exploiting the previously less available public education system.

NOTES

1. Ravitch, *The Troubled Crusade.*

2. ESEA, Section 6301, Part C (1)(A)(B), (2).

3. ESEA, Section 6305, Part(1)(2)(A)(B)(C)(D)(E)(i)(ii)(F)(G).

4. Retrieved from https://www.whitehouse.gov/blog/2009/07/24/president-race-top.

5. Christopher E. Edley. "Introduction: Lawyers and Education Reform," Harvard Journal on Legislation, 28(1991), 293.

6. Noam Chomsky, *Hegemony or Survival.*

7. Ravitch, *The Troubled Crusade.*

8. Retrieved from http://jaypgreene.com/2011/09/21/my-testimony-on-national-standards-before-us-house/.

9. Andrew Porter et al., "Common Core State Standards."

10. The Trouble with the Common Core. Retrieved from http://www.rethinking-schools.org/archive/27_04/edit274.shtml.

Chapter 7

A Study in Misrepresentation

Scholarly Interpretations of Policy Talk

While many policy reports and resulting legislative actions take care to present its impetuses and justifications in terms of "facts," or at least "scientific findings," the general precariousness of data in social science, especially when they are coupled with political motive, is considerable. An important factor to consider when analyzing such data is whether such "facts" are, indeed, factual or whether they are skewed, decontextualized, or even fabricated to serve a specific political agenda. In many, if not most cases in educational policy reporting, findings that are purported as "facts" are generally more representative of narrow and incomplete interpretations of dubiously devised statistical analyses, often suffering from multiple gaps either left unaccounted for and diverted from attention or filled with rhetoric in the form of commentary on the statistic itself emphatically presented as if it were fact.

Even clearer is the notion that the authors of such policy reports in education almost always represent either "outsiders" to the field of education or deliberately chosen "experts" that are expected to present findings according to a particular viewpoint, one that is often self-serving and closely matches the thrust of the reform campaign itself, as well as the political views of its proponents. That is, the simultaneous and often contraindicative findings of true educational experts or legitimate researchers are often entirely disregarded or, if heeded at all, distorted to fit the political agenda out of which the reform framework developed.

Exacerbating this dearth of expert contribution to the political discussions of educational reform is the fact that literature produced by legitimate researchers is often only accessible and of interest to other experts in the field, most of whom also have little, if any, access to policymakers or clout in the final versions of educational policies and legislation. As Cuban and Tyack suggest, education reform, as well as its potential failure suggests corruption of a noble dream by bureaucrats who consult narrow institutional interests, or their own self-interest, rather than the public good ... symbolic gestures, and the overpromising that accompanies them, have at times interested policymakers more than substance.[1]

Nation at Risk is an exemplary frame in which such a discussion of rhetorical distortion and decontextualized statistics of the state of education for explicit political use could begin. Richard Rothstein, a prominent educational commentator and skeptic of legislative reforms and governmental reports such as *Nation at Risk* has offered a number of critical interpretations since its original publication, generally indicating three major flaws of the *Nation at Risk* endeavor.[2]

First, the report erroneously concluded that student achievement was declining based on SAT scores, a largely unreliable measure of either aptitude or achievement, and an incomplete analysis of the National Assessment of Educational Progress (NAEP), a potentially stronger indicator should it have been analyzed more carefully and systematically. Second, the report placed a disproportionate amount of blame on the schools for problems over which they had little, if any, control or influence, a concept which had been convincingly demonstrated by the Coleman Report in 1966.[3] Third, but not likely finally, the report ignored other social and economic institutions for learning such as the church and the home.

Through this "doomsday aura"[4] the reporters engaged rhetoric rather than true data analysis in order to justify the need for education reform as a means of protecting the economic well-being of the country. Thus, the reporters capitalized on reinforcing a popular though hyperbolic and largely synthetic connection to global competitiveness, if not dominance. According to Cremin, these connections amounted to little more than an "ideological smokescreen" as he states:

American economic competitiveness ... is to a considerable degree a function of monetary, trade, and industrial policy, and of decisions made by the president and Congress, the Federal Reserve Board, and the Federal Departments of Treasury, Commerce, and Labor. Therefore, to conclude that problems of international competitiveness can be solved by educational reform, especially educational reform defined solely as school reform is not merely utopian and millenialist, it is at best foolish and at worst a crass effort to direct attention away from those truly responsible for doing something about competitiveness and to lay burden to the schools.[5]

The political motivation of such reports and its corresponding social and cultural messages must also not be ignored. At the time of its release, Ed Meese, Reagan's attorney general, strongly objected to the acceptance of

Nation at Risk despite support from other White House insiders, especially James Baker, Reagan's chief of staff, Mike Deaver, Reagan's close advisor, and T.H. Bell, the Secretary of Education who initially sanctioned the effort.

Despite the report's recycling of more of the same education reform rhetoric such as more rigorous standards, more curricular focus in science and mathematics, and more teacher training based on cherry-picked and decontextualized testimony and careless analysis of statistics,[6] the report was successful in initiating what was to become a multiple-decade (and continuing) war waged on public education, and one which would set several disturbing precedents allowing the slow but steady increase of private interest, influence, and control in public education.

Additional political "trickery" took place in 1990 when a report compiled by engineers at Sandia National Laboratories in Albuquerque, New Mexico, presented contradictory evidence to that of *Nation at Risk*, indicating that though there were, indeed, flaws within the educational system, there was no indication of systemic problems to the degree indicated by *Nation at Risk*. When the paper was submitted for publication it was quashed by multiple representatives of the Department of Education including then Deputy Secretary of Education David Kearns, a former CEO of Xerox, and then Assistant Secretary of Education Diane Ravitch, who has currently become one of the most prominent champions of the anti-corporate and anti-standardization movement, representing a bold ideological reversal.[7]

But the connections between George H.W. Bush's America 2000 and its preponderance, if not dominance, of corporate advisors and the current system of the Common Core State Standards facilitated under the Obama administration are not accidental and are, in fact, the outcome of a long and calculated plan to increase, and eventually cede, control and financing of public institutions to private corporate entities. They are, indeed, the culmination of both neoconservative and neoliberal efforts to systematically usurp power from the public and redistribute it to the policy elites, namely the corporate lobby.

One fact remained clear between the original 1965 passage of Elementary and Secondary Education Act (ESEA) and its reauthorization as No Child Left Behind (NCLB) in 2001: all efforts were entirely ineffective, and there were no discernible improvements in any areas cited. Martin and McClure (1969) reported, based on their study funded by the National Association for the Advancement of Colored People (NAACP) Legal Defense Fund, that most monies provided to the schools under Title I were misused. In general, most administrations included in the report regarded the funding that they received to invest in specific programs for the underserved as part of their general budget.[8] Later, in 1984, a longitudinal study by Carter showed that, despite some evidence of initial improvement of students in Title I schools as compared to their non-Title I counterparts (more in math than in reading, and more in elementary than in middle school), these gains were not sustainable over time.[9]

A 1997 study by Abt Associates, which analyzed data from roughly 40,000 students, suggested that there were still no discernible differences in academic performance between Title I and non-Title I students.[10] With all of the above-mentioned impetuses for educational reform combined leading to a clear demonstration of inefficacy, the "voluntary" nature of adopting common standards and allowing unfettered state control appeared to be a vast mistake.

By 2001 it was clear that there was a high rate of state noncompliance with Improving America's Schools Act regulations, especially in the area of the misuse of finances, specifically concerning monies earmarked for low-income children, most of which never reached them, making any potential resulting narrowing of the achievement gap impossible, if it were even probable to begin with. To boot, such violations for misuse of funds were not penalized to any degree. NCLB purported to make an earnest attempt to effectively oversee such compliance, thus promising to yield the progress that had remained unattained thereunto through a tighter system of accountability at all levels.

Despite actual increased oversight as well as well-documented indications of "lowering" standards to rig achievement scores and avoid federal penalty, comparisons between local and state tests and the NAEP continued to reveal that students were not achieving to proficient levels despite the reports of improvement provided by many states. As a result, an option was offered to families, and one that was to be opposed by many people on many fronts: the increased establishment of charter schools, cloaked as "school choice" and its resultant private interest and involvement in the public school system.

Beginning with the implementation of "vouchers," whereby parents would be able to remove their children from underperforming schools and send them to high-achieving ones, the notion of school choice and, essentially, competition with traditional public schools by "innovative" public schooling endeavors was set in full swing. Interestingly, this notion received bipartisan support, deepening the connection of private corporate interest in public policy for both neoliberal and neoconservative politicians.

This unanimous support also served to raise suspicion over the possibility of potential financial gain by a more discerning public, either in terms of political campaigning or personal wealth as a result of such an increase in educational commerce. But again, despite these efforts and its accompanying promises of change, an increasing amount of studies continued to reveal that the lofty goals set by NCLB was nowhere near achievement and may have even exacerbated the situation.[11]

In 2008, newly elected president Barack Obama, trailed by his litany of radical campaign promises, was now being confronted with the still failing but long-standing education reform initiatives that followed him into his presidency. Unable to attain the unprecedentedly partisan Congress to reauthorize the ESEA, still called NCLB, Obama was in a quandary as to how to move his educational reform platform forward. In one of his first novel uses of political maneuvering, Obama infused nearly $90 billion into educational initiatives as part of the aforementioned historic *American Reinvestment and Recovery Act* (ARRA), of which roughly $4.5 billion was earmarked for competitive state grants that would address the pernicious achievement gap known as Race to the Top (RTT).

Essentially, RTT was an initiative consisting entirely of "carrots" without any "sticks." By infusing the key tenets of previous educational reform, especially those of accountability, increased standards, teacher quality and compensation, and failing school reform, RTT virtually forced all states to design and, in some cases, implement policies along these lines regardless of whether they were going to actually receive monies from the grant. As a result, a crafty means of inserting federal influence in education without even the promise of funding was harnessed.

Contemporaneously, two powerful and politically connected organizations, the National Governors Association (NGA) and the Council of Chief State School Officers (CCSSO) organized a consortium of "educational experts" in English Language Arts and Mathematics in order to establish a set of "benchmarks" that states could adopt on a voluntary basis. With a curiously rapid formulation period followed by an equally rapid publication period, these two organizations released a final version of the "benchmarks," soon to be known as the Common Core State Standards (CCSS), in June 2010.[12]

In order to exert influence on the states to adopt the CCSS, the stipulations of RTT were changed to provide automatic "points" for states who indicated adoption of CCSS as part their grant applications. Before the August, 2010 RTT application deadline, 39 states had announced their plan to adopt CCSS, with virtually all of the rest following shortly thereafter.[13] While it is clear that governmental factions and policy elites were eager to comply with the mandates of RTT in order to maximize their chance for being granted funds, many social and educational organizations, including the NAACP, various state labor unions and the greater National Education Association (NEA) were expressing their disquiet with RTT, causing NEA going so far as to passing a vote of "no confidence" on behalf of their 3.2 million person membership.[14]

Among the most concerning of the critiques was the notion that for those states that did not receive monies from the grant, the most needy students would suffer even more of a disparity in educational support from those children in the states who did receive monies. This financial disparity is likely to actually deepen and widen the achievement gap as a direct result of a faulty, inequitable, and vastly unfair initiative claiming to seek to narrow it. This problem called into question the very ingenuity of the effort itself, and whether it ever possessed a true spirit of education reform or, more likely, provided a legislative means for marketization of the public school system.

Additionally, the reliance on charter schools and connecting student test scores with teacher evaluation measures in both the absence of curricular investment and the pressure of a tight deadline for compliance could, and in many states' cases did, result in haphazard, invalid, and unethical implementation of teacher evaluation. This concern was shared by the National Research Council (NRC), among other educational organizations, which released their own independent findings indicating that test-based incentive programs have been largely ineffective nationwide. Furthermore, they have not brought the United States into closer competition with the highest achieving countries, and omnipresent goal of all American educational legislation.[15]

Essentially, despite its innovative funding efforts and "green-lighting" of increased corporate influence and policymaking latitude, RTT appears to have committed the same historical sin of overpromising while under-delivering. However, while the initial failure of RTT may be dismissed by some politically invested individuals as a generally sound policy that simply needs "tweaking," the emotional fallout of parents, teachers, and, most importantly, students nationwide as a result of increased testing demands and unrealistic curricular changes based on the invalidated and rushed process of the CCSS could be the effort's most noxious legacy. And it is one that is apt to continue so long as the historical relevance of educational reform is not recognized soon by those in the policy elite.

NOTES

1. Cuban and Tyack, *Tinkering Toward Utopia,* 60–61.

2. Richard Rothstein, "A Nation at Risk Twenty-Five Years Later." CATO Unbound. (2005): Retrieved from http://www.cato-unbound.org/2008/04/07/richard-rothstein/nation-risk-twenty-five-years-later.

3. http://nysa32.nysed.gov/edpolicy/research/res_essay_johnson_cole.shtml.

4. Rothstein, "Twenty Five Years Later."

5. Lawrence Cremin, as cited by Gerald W. Bracey, "April Foolishness: The 20th Anniversary of a Nation at Risk" *Phi Delta Kappan,* 84 no. 8, (2003): 616–621.

6. Ibid.

7. Ibid.

8. Joseph P. Vittieri, *Choosing Equality: School Choice, the Constitution, and Civil Society.* Washington, D.C.: Brookings Institution Press, 2012.

9. Launor F. Carter. "The Sustaining Effects Study of Compensatory and Elementary Education." *Educational Researcher,* 13 no. 7, (1984): 4–13.

10. Vittieri, "Choosing Equality."

11. Ibid.

12. Retrieved from http://www.corestandards.org/about-the-standards/development-process/.

13. Vittieri, "Choosing Equality."

14. Ibid.

15. Ibid.

Chapter 8

Schooling and the "Culturally Deprived"

Racism and American Schooling

The deep-seated and contemporarily vilified practice of segregation and schooling is perhaps one of America's most regrettable legacies. That is, legacy if one believes that it is, indeed, a historical relic with no continuing legitimacy. While the current state of integration (or perhaps more aptly redistributed segregation) is a deeply complex historical, sociological, economic, and political issue that deserves immensely careful attention, there is no argument that the existence of racial segregation can be traced back to the very founding of America and the beginning of the American experiment.

It is also important to distinguish the somewhat pervasive fiction that segregation was endemic to the South, while the North ever-maintained a system of equal accessibility across races. This distinction is often contextualized through the notion of de jure segregation, or segregation mandated by law, and de facto segregation, which is segregation that is socially and culturally maintained in practice and is, in many ways, just as pernicious, if not more so.[1]

The question of separating white from black students can be traced back to a black veteran of the Revolutionary War, Prince Hall, who became a prominent community leader in the new republic. Noting the problems with the quality of what little schooling was provided at the time, Hall suggested that integration of black and white students was the cause of the inadequacy.[2] The reason Hall questioned the legitimacy of integrated schools was the vast difference between "African" culture and the newly forming "American" (i.e., white American) culture. According to Hall, "We ... must fear for our rising offspring to see them in ignorance in a land of gospel light."[3] This captures one of the lasting questions in the matter of integration: Do black children and white share enough common culture to be educated in a universally culturally relevant way?

In 1806 Hall's efforts for separate schooling proved successful, and the first school for black children was opened in Boston, Massachusetts. However, by 1835 there were growing complaints that the quality of instruction in the new school for the black students was poor, especially as compared to that of their white counterparts. Though these complaints resonated enough to result in the construction of a new school building for the black students, the lingering influence of racist policymaking by the centralized Boston School Committee maintained the ineffective and inequitable practices for the children despite the monetary investment.

In *Life and History in our Schools*,[4] Carter G. Woodson provides a deep examination of how black educational lives have progressed (or, more aptly, regressed) since the post–Civil War era. As Woodson explains, the initial reaction to the newly freed blacks by the abolitionist-minded whites was one of admiration and sympathy, those of a people who had been deeply oppressed by an inherently hateful and racist society at the behest of wealthy white men purely for the purpose of capitalistic gain.

With the largely failed effort of "Reconstruction" in the South, many of the politically powerful men of the time gradually reached a different conclusion: that the white men, despite their questionably moral actions of the past, had been mistreated and misunderstood, if not entirely misrepresented in the popular narrative. As a result, the newly freed black men and women were no longer the focus of attention and "reconstruction," but rather reduced to the "status of the free Negro prior to the Civil War on the grounds that it had been proved the he was not a white man with black skin."[5]

The pervasive consequence of this transformed perception was the perpetuation of the decontextualized and largely fictitious "southern White man's" story of the ubiquitous "Black man." Though diluted in some ways in the northern states' curricula, the general narrative was maintained in terms of cultural representation, maintaining the general caricature of the black person. That is, since the freed blacks of the south (as well as the "always free" blacks of the north) had not gained social and economic prominence despite their freedom by the early 20th century, there must have been some sort of biological, if not hereditary explanation for such a failure. The social result was nearly omnipresent: segregation, at best, and denial of education and overt subjugation, at worst.

The inequity of the differences between segregated schools in both the north and the south became clear and was widely vocalized by the famed abolitionist lawyer Charles Sumner in 1850. According to him:

> The separation of the schools, so far from being for the benefit of both races, is an injury to both. It tends to create a feeling of degradation in the blacks, and of prejudice and uncharitableness [sic] in the whites.[6]

As a result Sumner, assisted by a number of black lawyers, filed suit against the school system of the city of Boston on behalf of Benjamin Roberts, whose daughter Sarah was refused admission to four schools closer to her home than the one she was permitted to attend simply on the basis of race. Describing the rationale of the case Sumner suggests:

> The school is the little world in which the child is trained for the larger world of life, beginning there those relations of Equality which the constitution and the laws promise to all. ... I conclude there is little but one kind of public school, free to all, whether rich or poor, whether Catholic or Protestant, whether White or Black—excluding none, comprehending all.[7]

Though reaching the Supreme Court of Massachusetts only to suffer the ultimate dismissal of the case by Chief Justice Lemuel Shaw, the integrationist activists redirected their pursuit of the issue to the Massachusetts legislature. This campaign was vastly more successful, resulting in the ruling that segregation was unconstitutional and therefore abolished in the state of Massachusetts. While seemingly a victory at face value, one of the more important lessons of the imminent Civil Rights Movement was prophesied in Sumner's Massachusetts case: that in the spirit of compliance with the integrationist law, black schools were closed leading to a massive loss of jobs for those black teachers, as well as the elimination of financial assistance that was provided to the black students so long as they attended black schools. The integrationist movement was thus presented with a pernicious paradox that was to haunt it for many years to come.

The rallying cry of black leaders such as Frederick Douglass and the later emerging W.E.B. DuBois was largely consistent; however, the question of equality was not in the schools themselves, but rather in the purpose that the schools, through their provision of education, served. As suggested in DuBois's brilliant though pithy quip, "[the Negro child] needs neither segregated schools nor mixed schools. What he needs is education."[8] That is, regardless of where such education is provided and among whom, education is to be seen as the most powerful liberating force to securing the freedom and social justice that is rightful to black people in America.

Despite the precedent in the law established by *Plessy v. Ferguson* (1896), which validated the constitutionality of "separate but equal" NAACP set out on a systematic effort to dismantle this fallacious basis for segregation beginning in the 1930s. In 1950, as a product of their research and efforts, 13 black parents residing in the area of Topeka, Kansas, were advised by a team of lawyers from the NAACP to attempt to enroll their children in neighborhood white schools that were geographically closer to their homes than the schools their children attended. This strategy mimicked a tactic first used in the aforementioned Roberts case. Expectedly, as all children were denied the opportunity to enroll in these schools, the lawyers filed an initial class action suit on behalf of the families against the City of Kansas in the District Court.

Having initially lost the case due to the upholding of the *Plessy v. Ferguson* precedent, the NAACP successfully petitioned their case to be heard by the US Supreme Court in what was to become one of the most dramatic instances of arguing for racial equality under the law in the history of the United States. In a unanimous decision released on May 17, 1954, Chief Justice Earl Warren declared:

> It is doubtful that any child may reasonably be expected to succeed in life if he is denied the opportunity to an education. Such an opportunity ... is a right which must be made available to all on equal terms ... separate educational facilities are inherently unequal.[9]

Though the legal initiative toward desegregation was set in motion, the social response was far from abiding. Increased tension between races, especially in the south where de jure segregation was simply regarded as an accepted and necessary part of the culture, was ever-present and growing.

There was also an increase in legal "loopholing" as well as outright defiance of the new mandate. For example, Omer Carmichael, the superintendent of the Louisville, Kentucky, schools put forth a desegregation plan which included a transfer option for 85 percent of affected white students as well as setting the definition of "racially mixed" as the presence of "at least one negro." No act of outright defiance, however, was as clear as that of Governor Orville Faubus of Arkansas who boldly claimed:

> I will not force my people to integrate against their will. I believe in the democratic processes and principles of government wherein the people determine the problems on a local level, which is their right.[10]

While many opposing integration as per Brown cloaked their opposition within the context of the federal government overstepping bounds and interfering in a state-run entity such as schooling, the racial issue itself was quite clearly what was problematic to the opposition. Faubus's noncompliance remains as one of the most memorialized scenes from the Civil Rights Movement in which nine black children (eventually known as the "Little Rock Nine") entered the schoolhouse escorted by members of the National Guard as well as the 101st Airborne.

Neither desegregation nor integration appeared to really be the reparative maneuver that society needed. As Melba Patillo Beale, one of the "Little Rock Nine," laments in her autobiography:

Back then, I naively believed that if we could end segregation in the schools, all barriers of inequality would fall. If you had asked in 1957 what I expected, I would have told you that by this time [1994] our struggle for human rights would have been won.[11]

Black children were simply not welcome in white schools. That is, it was not segregation itself that was the problem, but rather the underlying hatred and bigotry that fostered a cultural and social system that was able to continually justify it that was. As James Anderson explains:

[The black children's] sense was, we are going into an environment where we are not wanted. The teachers are going to be hostile. The students think of us as a despised race. We cannot make friends. We will be isolated and discriminated against. And the question for African Americans is, do you want your children to pioneer this process? Do you want your children to pay this price?[12]

The sentiment of "integration" was also never the true goal of the Brown plaintiffs at a social level. According to Vivian Scales, one of the plaintiffs in the class action:

It wasn't that we wanted our children to go to a school with white children. That was not the gist of it at all. We wanted our children to have a better and equal education, which we knew they were not getting.[13]

This concern was present even before the Brown decision. During the Truman administration when the debate over the appropriateness of the federal government's provision of money for schools was at its most fervent, the issue of whether segregated schools should receive such funds arose. That is, should the Truman administration, one that was generally more liberal and less favorable toward segregation, use federal funding of schools as leverage for desegregation? While a number of proponents as well as opponents battled over this question from a purely political position, there was an ever-growing sense of the illogic of the idea. As Rabbi Roland Gittelsohn famously declared:

I am deeply disturbed by this notion that by putting more money and better teachers into a segregated school system in the south you will thereby take an appreciable step toward the eventual elimination of segregation. You won't. Children don't learn from books, but from the life they are living, and the basic truth of a southern educational system lies not in what you teach but in the fact that the white the child knows that the colored child isn't good enough to go to school with him."[14]

A deep sense of American hypocrisy regarding race was also felt by the black soldiers returning from World War II. The idea that the American government was promulgating their role in the preservation of justice around the world while their own country was deeply entrenched in a system of institutional bigotry became a real threat to nationalism. This was especially true from a group of veterans who had either died or served in battle on behalf of that very country which systematically excluded them upon their return.[15]

An additional consequence of desegregation resulting from Brown was of a significant economic hardship to the black community, and one that was foreshadowed by the Roberts case in Boston. That is, while black schools were being closed in order to facilitate integration into white schools, nearly 30,000 black teachers and staff either lost their jobs or were displaced. This result acts as but another example of the notion that desegregation appeared to be less about progressing morally toward equality in the society, and more in terms of responding to a social demand of a people without truly exercising and applying its ethical undertones.

The integration effort resulting from Brown was a pivotal moment for the growing field of social science as well as an opportunity for an experiment in the inherence of elitism in American society. In 1964 a consortium of prominent social scientists met at the University of Chicago to discuss the notion of "cultural deprivation" and its effect, or at least correlation with, on education.

While the term "culturally deprived" was clearly a euphemistic description for poor black children, this meeting acted as a catalyzing agent for what would become the widespread neoliberal social movement. That is, enhancing the idea of social melioration while maintaining the elitism of the dominant class (i.e., the white male). This notion of maintaining hegemony while acting charitably is a common occurrence in the domain of educational reform, even contemporarily. By recognizing one's "deficiency" and seeking to "repair" it through either governmentally or socially sanctioned interventions, members of the dominant class are able to maintain their elitism as well as perpetuate the illusion of social awareness and melioration. As Shelby Steele suggests:

> By relegating the good to the government, and making it a matter of public policy [Americans] transformed [the good] from an earnest and personal moral struggle into a glib cultural symbolism. ... Americans could navigate around any guilt over the past simply by acquiescing to governmental interventions.[16]

But this is exactly the course that the initial attempts to end "cultural deprivation" took.

Quite systematically, especially as established by Title I of the Elementary and Secondary Education Act under Johnson in 1965, which infused an unprecedented amount of federal aid into the school system, a fully sponsored governmental effort to rehabilitate black children was underway. This approach of social amelioration through governmental action was grounded squarely in a deficit model. Within this framework, black children were seen as "deficient" and in need of "rehabilitation" to a higher standard. This cultural mind-set was to set a seemingly indelible precedent, if not centricity, in education reform legislation. As Frank Riessman comments:

> It would be easy to say, as many have said, that we must give these children what middle-class parents give their children—we must stimulate them in the use of language through reading, discussion, and the like. However, it is probably that this would not work, nor would it make the best use of the deprived child's particular mode of functioning ... we must be careful to not try to make these children into replicas of middle class children.[17]

So it becomes clear that the power of the middle-class ethos has been maintained in the establishment, construction, and many iterations of reconstruction that the American public school has undergone. The purpose of schooling then, appears not to truly be to provide education for young minds in order to keep them civically engaged and in control of their own liberation and freedom. Rather, it is to embed the value system of the white middle class as the cultural standard and use it as the litmus for judging one's "includability" and accessibility to the mainstream society.

The ideas of the deficit model and the need for the rehabilitation of deprived children will become pivotal over the decades following Lyndon B. Johnson "Great Society," and will ultimately blaze the path by which corporations and policy elites are allowed, by virtue of capitalism and political corruption, to veritably "buy" America's public schools. This process served the purpose of all but solidifying the capitalistic functioning of schooling in America. The clear result was the engraining, from the very beginning of the acculturation process, the notions of classism, racism, sexism, and ableism, all of which are exploited by the power and policy elites to maintain their hegemonic position in a deeply stratified society.

NOTES

1. Jason Sokol, *All Eyes are Upon Us: Race and Politics from Boston to Brooklyn* (New York: Basic Books, 2015).

2. Derrick Bell, "The Legacy of W.E.B. DuBois: A Rational Model for Achieving Public School Equity for America's Black Children." *Creighton Law Review*, 11 (1978): 409–431.

3. Ibid.

4. Carter G. Woodson, "Negro Life and History in our Schools." *The Journal of Negro History*, 4 no. 3, (1919): 273–280.

5. Ibid., p. 274.

6. Sumner, as cited in Bell, 412.

7. Mondale, *School*, 45.

8. DuBois, as cited in Bell, 415.

9. U.S. 483, 74 S.Ct.686, 98 L.Ed. 873, 38 A.L.R.2d 1180.

10. Patton, *School,* 142.

11. Ibid., 127.

12. Ibid., 143–144.

13. Ibid., 137.

14. Ravitch, *The Troubled Crusade*, 23.

15. Ibid.

16. Shelby Steele, *Shame How America's Past Sins Have Polarized our Country* (New York: Basic Books, 2015), 128.

17. Frank Riessman, as cited by Ravitch, *The Troubled Crusade,* 155.

Chapter 9

White Flight and Black Plight
Situating the Segregated Neighborhood

There have been many rhetorical and "paper tiger" initiatives forwarded to correct the systematic racism that is seemingly inherent in American social practice and tacit in American social policy. Still, there is much to be said about the pervasiveness of segregation despite such putative social and legislative interest in its amelioration. The Civil Rights Act of 1965 provides a strong foundation upon which this contradictory state of affairs can be examined. According to Title VI of the Act:

> No person ... shall, on ground of race, color, national origin, be excluded from participation in, be denied the benefits of, or be subjected to discrimination under any program or activity receiving federal financial assistance.[1]

Coming only a decade after the Brown decision it appeared that there was, indeed, an earnest interest in ameliorating the racial stratification problem in American society. However, there is a distinct difference between forwarding legislation and mandating practice and genuinely addressing deep-seated cultural values and social mores. These values were so deep and valuable to some that they were, just a century before the Civil Rights Act's passage, deemed legitimate enough to add to the justification of a civil war and near separation of the union.

The existing desegregation actions combined with the initial Civil Rights Act of 1965 reveal one of the clearest contradictions in American society, and one that continues even in present day: the ability to support racial equality legislatively, with rousing self-congratulation, while continuing to permit middle- and upper-class American society to maintain racial segregation in their daily lives.

James S. Coleman in 1966, in a widely cited and catalytic research endeavor formally titled "Equal Education Opportunity" but known more widely as "the Coleman Report," first suggested the phenomenon of "white flight." In a similar criticism of the legislative effect on genuine social policy and practice, Coleman suggested that the various legislative attempts by the courts and the legislature, namely *Brown v. Board of Education* and the Civil Rights Act of 1965, actually exacerbated the state of race relations in America resulting not in integration, but rather re-segregation in a different pattern.

This pattern consisted of black "in-migration," or the movement of black families into predominantly white neighborhoods, especially in southern urban areas and northern territories, leading to white egression to other neighborhoods, which would then become predominantly white. Growing ever common, this clearly documented phenomenon of geographical displacement and replacement in a different geographical area as a result of black in-migration came to be known as "White flight." As Coleman suggests:

> The extremely strong reactions of individual whites in moving their children out of large districts engaged in massive and rapid desegregation suggests that in the long run the policies that have been pursued will defeat the purpose of increasing overall contact among races.[2]

The phenomenon of "white flight" is contemporaneous with the expanse of suburbanization, a phenomenon apparent in many urban areas, with some estimates indicating as many as two white departures for every one black arrival.[3,4] As a result, there has been a continual disproportionality of funding and private investment between predominantly white areas of affluence and predominantly black (and Latino) areas of socioeconomic challenge in both the south and the north.[5]

The phenomenon of "white flight" has appeared to remain consistent through the 1990s, with some studies indicating that white families will engage in white flight in response to an influx of poor black families to their neighborhoods as well as an adverse response to racial diversity in a school system, which is often associated with declining academic quality.[6] Evidence of white flight also appears to persist in the 21st century, potentially contributed to by the increasing availability of "school choice," a mandate of NCLB purportedly intending to increase opportunity for black and culturally diverse schoolchildren to receive quality education, but one that seems to have had the opposite effect. Other studies indicate that the emergence of more private school choice, as well as charter school options may add to the persistence of not only school segregation but "white flight" itself.[7]

The phenomenon of "white flight" makes it clear that despite the legislative efforts to increase desegregation by mandating practice, the deep-seated cultural trend toward racism and racial separation appears to remain pervasively intact, effectively subverting these efforts. This result begs the question: can the members of a society be legally mandated or compelled to act in opposition to a notion that is seemingly inherent to their cultural identity and social functioning? And, if not, what is the social and cultural impact of this inability? The answer in American society is clear: with "white flight" comes "black stagnancy."

The perpetual cultural notion that black people are morally and socially inferior to white people leads to the social logic that black neighborhoods are morally and socially degenerative to the greater culture as opposed to white neighborhoods, which are largely contributive. The notion of the "liberal" approach of remediation based on cultural deprivation is a testament to this notion, and indicative of the idea that the social referent for acceptable standards of living is that of the middle class, with failure to reach this standard equal to failure to fulfill the role of schooling and acculturation.

This issue remains one of the most pressing challenges of schooling among diverse individuals, especially since one of the main findings of the Coleman Report, as well as other reports since, has been that racial inequality and cultural disparities in schooling and academic achievement cannot be blamed entirely, or even predominantly, on the school or the educational process itself. Rather, a number of other significant pernicious social problems including family background, poverty, and competing social influences (such as criminal elements, gang affiliation, and mass incarceration, especially in urban or socioeconomically depressed suburban areas that are also predominantly black) are also largely contributive.

There are explanations, often proffered by those of the middle class, including the black middle class, which focus on stratification in terms of "classism"—that is, stratification between races is not a matter of racism (or a function of race itself), but rather a function of socioeconomic class. This point is often demonstrated through use of the black middle class and the social narrative of the continued success of black Americans who have overcome adversity and "gotten out" of the "ghetto." However, it begs revealing that the black middle class represents a rather small percentage of the black community. Additionally, its existence serves less in invalidating the issue of race, but more in validation of the notion of the superiority of middle-classism and the cultural, social, and economic importance of assimilation. That is, the existence of the black middle class is the exception that proves the rule. As Ogbu explains:

> A stratified society is a society in which there is a differential relationship between members of its constituent groups and the society's fundamental resources, so that some people (e.g., white Americans), by virtue of their

membership in particular social groups, have almost unimpaired access to the strategic resources, while some other people (e.g., black Americans), by virtue of their own membership in other social groups, have various impediments in their access to the same strategic fundamental resources. ... In a stratified society there is usually an overarching ideology ... embodying the dominant group's rationalizations or explanations of hierarchical ordering of the groups. Subordinate social groups do not necessarily accept the rationalizations of the system; however, they are not entirely free from its influence.[8]

Therefore, the school itself is not *the* sole instrument of stratification, but does, indeed, serve as a ubiquitous contributor to the propagation of social and cultural narratives of white America and its instillation among the black community, especially the black youth.

The school is, ultimately, the main institution of reinforcement of this idea of difference in value. When black children show up to dilapidated buildings, scarce and outdated materials, overcrowded classrooms, metal detectors at the entryway, inconsistent teaching and leadership, disproportionately harsh disciplinary practices and a generally disinterested public, the message becomes clear: *you are not worth the investment.* As Kumasi suggests:

The lack of opportunities for quality schooling [in predominantly black areas is] not a coincidence but, rather, can be attributed to the confluence of several social and economic forces that have played out over decades ... even centuries. ... Over the last twenty years ... one can discern a disturbing trend in mainstream educational discourses regarding how school inequities are explained. The tendency is to attribute the disparities that exist between inner-city and suburban school resources and between achievement among white and nonwhite youth to issues of class, while dismissing or minimizing the influence of racism.[9]

But in order to understand why *race* as a construct, as opposed to *class* as a grouping, is more significant than is often suggested from both liberal and conservative viewpoints, it is important to contextualize how race is actually constructed in a hegemonic society. According to Omi and Winant, race is

a process of historically situated *projects* [italics in original] in which human bodies and social structures are represented and organized ... [which links] ... racial formation to the evolution of hegemony, the way in which society is organized and ruled.[10]

It is the very function of race, in this context, that allows an entire set of people (most notably black Americans) to be continuously subjugated even in the face of the "social improvement" of specific individual or subgroup members (e.g., the black middle class or even the exceptional black millionaire outside of sports and entertainment). In many ways, the formation of the black middle class is a validation of the perniciousness of racial thinking, allowing those who wish to blame the state of the black community on personal failure to do so by pointing out the success of other "black counterparts" (i.e., if *they* did it, why can't *you* do it?).

In this sense, then, the notion of classism is inseparable from the notion of racism. Since the Constitution is, in many ways, regarded as the defining document in securing property rights and, therefore, the resulting "inalienable rights" for white male members of the new republic, the very lack of property ownership for black Americans provides for a fundamental exclusion from the very intention of the Constitution itself. The very fact that at the time of the Constitutional Convention and the subsequent ratification period black people were considered property themselves, and would be for nearly a century longer. Essentially, this entirely excluded them, as a group, from the notion of property ownership (property cannot own property). Property ownership then was something that white males (and their families by extension) only could enjoy, and reflected only the newly forming hegemonic white male American culture.[11]

In that, the color of an individual's skin became one of distinct systematic utility in political, governmental, and social processes, all of which black individuals were barred from. Race, from this perspective, fulfills Omi and Winant's criteria as a socio-historical tool to establish and maintain hegemony and allows for the systematic formation of racism in virtually all resulting public policies. Further social "clumping" of black individuals, regardless of their country of origin or purpose in America, provides much evidence to the social project conceptualization. That is, whether one was an immigrant business owner from Haiti or a visiting student from Nigeria, they were socially regarded, first and foremost, if not only, as black.

As a result of this deep-seated and highly pervasive notion of race throughout society and its resultant functions and processes, the notion of middle-classism is perpetually maintained as the cultural litmus by which all individuals can gauge their relative success and social acceptability. As Ladson-Billings suggests, in a society in which "whiteness" is positioned to be the norm, all members of the society are ranked and categorized in comparison to it.[12] That is, those individuals who progress in an economically and socially "normative" way (going to school, holding a "respectable" job, speaking appropriately, such as a black accountant, dentist, or doctor) are seen as culturally contributive (as compared to their relation to the middle-class white standard) as opposed to those who serve a less economically contributive and socially acceptable function (such as a fast-food restaurant worker, doorman, or cleaner).

The idea of "whiteness" then is the means by which the standard is preserved and pervaded, with the school being, in many ways, its main instrument. According to Swartz:

> Master scripting silences multiple voices and perspectives, primarily legitimizing dominant, white, upper-class, male voicings as the "standard" knowledge students need to know. All other accounts are omitted from the master script unless they can be disempowered through misrepresentation. Thus, content that does not reflect the dominant voice must be brought under control, *mastered* [italics in original], and then reshaped before it can become part of the master script.[13]

This view emphasizes the often sterilized versions of important race-based events from history such as that of Rosa Parks (and her portrayal as a "tired old woman"), the "civil disobedience" of Martin Luther King, Jr. (omitting his support of socialism and scathing critique of capitalism), and the nonviolence of Nelson Mandela (veritably erasing his militant early days) among a number of other grossly misrepresented historical accounts.[14]

This sterile version of history also serves a subjugating purpose. That is, by including blacks and Latinos as but another "immigrant culture" comparable to the Irish, the Italian, the Eastern European Jews, and others who have come in search of the "American Dream" and have largely achieved it, their failure to reach middle-classism as a group, and as a result of some sort of group deficiency, is reinforced. Absent from the narrative, however, is the very important fact that most black people's presence in the United States is a result of forced entry through slavery, not voluntary immigration. As a result, a sense of both social guilt and social blame is proffered, perpetuating the notion that such social failure must only be blamed on cultural defect, as all other groups managed to overcome adversity and attain the middle-class standard.[15]

One of the main efforts to address the issue of racial inequality through schooling has been the efforts of multicultural education, a relatively nebulous and often contentious term that is often erroneously used as a reference to the act of superimposing the idea of "righting" past "wrongs" in curricular representation. A consistency across multicultural education efforts, however, is the continual challenge toward assimilationist viewpoints and its more pointed focus on pluralism and egalitarianism. With these counter-narratives in place, multiculturalism aims at disembodying the dominant cultural in order to make room for more accurately culturally representative ones.[16]

The goal of such an approach, then, is to be simultaneously liberating for members of the school culture who identify with the represented cultures as well as demanding of respect and value by those who are not. At the heart of such an approach, however, is the call for systematic, cultural, institutional change that diminishes the stronghold of the hegemonic narrative and allows its influence to be replaced by genuine versions of those narratives that have been intentionally suppressed in the mainstream curriculum.[17]

Though there is a growing attention to multicultural education and its significance in addressing racial and ethnic stratification in American schools and greater society, there is still a fierce stronghold of white middle-class values that maintain control over the schools. Research from the beginning of the 21st century continues to indicate that schools remain even more segregated currently than they had been during the times of both de jure and de facto segregation. Some statistics indicate that, by and large, the vast majority of white students in America attend schools that are upwards of 80 percent white, while nearly two out of every five black and Latino students attend a school that is virtually entirely nonwhite, with nearly 99–100 percent of its student body black and Latino.[18,19] This amounts to little less than de facto apartheid in a country that is purported to be built upon freedom and equality for all.

NOTES

1. As cited by Ravitch, *The Troubled Crusade.*

2. James S. Coleman, "Recent Trends in School Integration," *Educational Researcher,* 4 no. 7, (1975), 3.

3. William H. Frey, "Central City White flight: Racial and Nonracial Causes." *American Sociological Review,* 44 no. 3, (1979): 425–448.

4. Leah Platt Bouston, "Was Postwar Suburbanization White flight? Evidence from the Black Migration." *The Quarterly Journal of Economics,* 125 no. 1, (2010): 417–443.

5. William H. Frey, "Black In-Migration, White flight, and the Changing Economic Base of the Central City." *American Journal of Sociology,* 85 no. 6, (1979): 1396–1417.

6. Robert W. Farlie and Alexandra M. Resch, "Is There 'White flight' into Private Schools? Evidence from the National Educational Longitudinal Survey." *The Review of Economics and Statistics,* 84 no. 1, (2002): 21–33.

7. Ibid.

8. John U. Ogbu, "Racial Stratification and Education in the United States: Why Inequality Persists." *Teachers College Record,* 96 no. 2, (1994): 264–298.

9. Kafi D. Kumasi, (2011). Critical Race Theory and Education: Mapping a Legacy of Scholarship and Activism." In Levinson, B.A.U. (Ed.), Beyond Critique: Critical Social Theories and Education (pp. 196–219). Boulder, CO: Paradigm Publishers.

10. Michael Omi and Howard Winant, *Racial Formation in the United States from the 1960s to the 1990s* (New York: Routledge, 1994), 9.

11. Cheryl I. Harris, "Whiteness as Property." *Harvard Law Review*, 106, (1993): 1721.

12. Gloria Ladson-Billings, "Just what is Critical Race Theory and What's it Doing in a *Nice* Field Like Education?" *Qualitative Studies in Education,* 11 no. 1, (1996): 7–24.

13. Swartz, 1992 as cited by Ladson-Billings. "Critical Race Theory."

14. Bill Ayers, *Public Enemy: Confessions of an American Dissident* (New York: Beacon, 2013).

15. Ladson-Billings, "Critical Race Theory."

16. Cameron McCarthy, "Rethinking Liberal and Radical Perspectives on Racial Equality in Schooling: Making the Case for Nonsynchrony." *Harvard Educational Review*, 58 (1988): 3.

17. James A. Banks, "Multicultural Education: Historical Development, Dimensions, and Practice." *Review of Research in Education*, 19 (1993): 3–49.

18. Erika Frankenberg, Chungmei Lee, and Gary Orfield , "A Multicultural Society with Segregated Schools: Are We Losing the Dream?" From http://escholarship.org/uc/item/3rh7w18g#page-1.

19. Gary Orfield, "Reviving the Goal of an Integrated Society: A 21st Century Challenge," 2009. From http://escholarship.org/uc/item/2bw2s608#page-13.

Chapter 10

Measuring Value

Intelligence Testing and the "Science" of Ability

In a capitalistic society such as America's, it is important to determine who or, in some cases, which groups are worth social and economic investment and which are not. However, it is difficult to determine how a society is to determine such worth for investment, be it public or private. This issue was less problematic before the early 20th century when segregation, be it de jure or de facto, was the way of life and there were few "unwanted" immigrants to consider. However, between 1900 and the mid-1920s, the ability to evaluate individual worth, especially in terms of economic contribution to the capitalist endeavor, became increasingly socially important.

With the influx of European immigrants from "less cultured" countries, such as those in Eastern Europe, as well as an increased interest in identifying and categorizing the "mentally deficient" (known also by a multitude of additional terms such as "feeble-minded," "dim-wit," and "moron/idiot/imbecile" as actual clinical designations), the growing American economy was perceived by much of the public to have been facing a major threat by allowing the introduction of such "undesirables" into the country.

In the early 1900s French psychologists Alfred Binet and Theodore Simon began to theorize about the nature of human intelligence. Believing that intelligence was a learned entity, as opposed to a heritable one, Binet and Simon developed an assessment in 1905 (later revised in 1908 and again in 1911) which they believed could capture the current level of one's intelligence. The assessment consisted of 30 cognitive scales presented in a hierarchical order of complexity, which putatively measured aspects of one's intelligence such as language skills, memory, reasoning, digit span, and psychophysical judgments (later re-conceptualized as spatial reasoning).[1] These tests, Binet and Simon suggested, could measure a child's current intellectual level. This conceptualization was to prove a lasting one, now referred to as one's "mental age."

The original intent of the scale was to determine which students were functioning at "lower levels" than their expected "intellectual level" (based on their age) and would therefore require remediation. That is, the test was not designed to define and categorize those with "mental deficiency" to justify some sort of exclusion, but rather act as a screening tool in order to determine for whom additional instruction was likely needed.

However, when Henry Goddard, a well-known American physician and staunch eugenicist, learned of the scale while traveling in Europe, he obtained a version of it. He soon adapted it to be used as an evaluation tool for the children at the Training School at Vineland, a residential facility for children with "cognitive disorders" for which he served as director. Within only a few years, a translated version of the Binet-Simon scale was being used to evaluate children across America.

Shortly before the United States entered World War I, the Binet-Simon scale underwent two distinct revisions by prominent American psychologists. First, Robert Yerkes and James Bridges adapted the scale from a "year metric" to a "point metric" by revising the groupings of the individual subtests. Second, Lewis Terman, an American psychologist at Stanford University, revised the test by extending its application into adulthood, adding additional tests, modifying administration methods and material (such as using foam boards), and, perhaps most importantly, converting the measure of "mental age" into a new measure he termed an "intelligence quotient" (IQ).[2]

Responding to the need for more adaptable forms of intelligence tests for instances in which an individual either could not understand verbal language (in the case of an intellectual disability or what would contemporarily be called autism) or did not understand English (in the case of immigrants from non-English-speaking countries), other psychologists designed nonverbal intelligence tests, such as the Pictorial Completion Tests by Healy (1921) and the Leiter International Performance Scale (1929). Finally, David Wechsler, upon becoming the chief psychologist at the Bellevue Psychiatric Hospital of New York, further innovated the practice of intelligence testing by incorporating both verbal and performance tests into one comprehensive assessment, which would eventually become the nearly ubiquitous Wechsler scales with versions for preschoolers, children, and adults.

The use of intelligence tests to evaluate individuals for a number of purposes became commonplace in early 20th-century American society, and would come to serve a number of different purposes ranging from justifying institutionalization for the "feeble-minded" to limiting immigration from particular countries to maintaining the idea of genetic superiority of the white race. As expressed by Stephen Jay Gould in his now classic book *The*

Mismeasure of Man regarding his refutation of the IQ theory (specifically with regard to Herrnstein and Murray's controversial book *The Bell Curve*):

> [IQ] is about the abstraction of intelligence as a single entity, its location within the brain, its quantification as one number for each individual, and the use of these numbers to rank people in a single series of worthiness, invariably to find that oppressed and disadvantaged groups—races, classes, sexes—are innately inferior and deserve their status.[3]

Despite these "advances" in mental measurement, the nature and meaning of intelligence as a construct remained unclear, and this discrepancy would serve a very important function in the provision of educational services for a variety of children over the 20th and 21st centuries. With the debate over the conceptualization of intelligence beginning as early as the development of intelligence tests themselves, this discussion has remained deeply fervent in the fields of psychology and education. Even as early as 1927, within the very first 20 years of the development of basic cognitive assessment, psychologist Charles Spearman suggested that the word "intelligence" had become a "mere vocal sound, a word with so many meanings that finally it has none."[4] Similar sentiments have been suggested by a number of well-known contemporary intellectuals and psychologists since including Arthur Jensen, Robert Sternberg, and Howard Gardner.

The issue became so pressing in current social science scholarship and practice that in November 1994 the Board of Scientific Affairs of the American Psychological Association (APA) convened a committee to address the varying conceptualizations of intelligence in order to fulfill an "urgent need for an authoritative report on these issues—one that all sides could use as a basis."[5] The consortium sought to investigate the two main discrepancies regarding the concept of intelligence: (1) the general interpretations of the concept of intelligence and (2) the general interpretations of the state of psychometric instrumentation for measuring intelligence.

Regarding the first question, the committee suggested that for those who believe in the psychometric capabilities of intelligence, the two main measures were the intelligence quotient (IQ) as per Terman and *g* (general intelligence), originally proposed by Charles Spearman though studied and revised conceptually by a number of cognitive theorists.[6] Regarding the second question, the committee suggested that while there are a number of intellectuals who cite research supporting the validity and reliability of the psychometric approach to measuring intelligence, there are a number who make compelling arguments to the contrary.

Jean Piaget, one of the most indispensable scholars of child development, contributed much counter-theory to the psychometric conception of

intelligence. Piaget, dissimilarly from many of the contemporaneous thinkers on intelligence, focused little on individual differences. Rather, Piaget
stressed the universality of child development through common processes
of assimilating and accommodating new information into existing cognitive
structures.

In order to assess these growing conceptualizations, Piaget devised constructivist based tasks, which focused on "coming to" conclusions via activities. One classic example of a Piagetian conceptual test was pouring water
from a tall beaker to a stout beaker and evaluating whether or not the amount
of water remained constant. The idea behind these Piagetian tests were theoretically opposed to predetermined "cognitive" tasks that were divorced from
practical application, formative observation, and engagement.

It was through these types of investigations that Piaget believed his theories could be supported. This difference in the very fundamental notion of
how an idea is supported or evidenced in Piaget's theoretical framework is
an important counterpoint to consider in response to the commonly leveled
critique that Piagetian theory has not been supported by empirical evidence.[7]
That is, Piagetian theory has always been far more qualitative in conceptualization and assessment than quantitative, the main modality of measuring and
conceptualizing most contemporary notions of intelligence.

Lev Vygotsky, a Russian learning theorist who also conceptualized child
development quite differently than the IQ theorists, expressed his theory
largely through the construct he termed the "zone of proximal development"
(ZPD). According to Vygotsky, ZPD can be defined as:

> The distance between the actual development level as determined by indepen-
> dent problem solving and the level of potential development as determined
> through problem solving under adult guidance or in collaboration with more
> capable peers.[8]

Therefore, the child learns in ways that necessitate help at the beginning
of acquisition and result in increased independence through practice and
guidance. As such, for both Vygotsky and Piaget, intelligence served a very
practical problem-solving function and was best assessed in the context of
"real tasks" with practical and functional results. Metrics that were based
more so on simulated and decontextualized tests within largely synthesized
quantitative products were believed to be far less useful or suited to capture
intelligence from the constructivist perspective.

Howard Gardner, one of the most prominent contemporary vocal opponents to the traditional notion of intelligence as a fixed and measurable factor,
proposed an alternative concept of "multiple intelligences." The main criticism Gardner makes of conceptualizing intelligence based on "normative"

scales is its bias toward other individuals who are "non-normative." These "non-normative" individuals include savants, virtuosos, gifted persons, or persons with brain damage (acquired or congenital) or neurological disability or difference.

By using normative comparisons, Gardner argues, intelligence tests are only able to approximate values of linguistic, logical, and some aspects of spatial intelligence, virtually ignoring many other legitimate contributive factors. Further, such tests risk ignoring practical uses of intelligence that cannot be captured by psychometric assessments such as spontaneous language use as a factor of verbal ability and the ability to find one's way in a new town as a factor of spatial ability. Gardner's theory has received much attention, both in support and opposition in terms of both its practicality and empirical support.[9,10]

Robert Sternberg, a second contemporary vocal opponent to the conventional theory of intelligence argues mainly against the unilateral nature of the psychometric concept of intelligence. According to Sternberg, intelligence is better captured in terms of a "triarchic" approach: analytic, creative, and practical.

In Sternberg's critique, only the first part, analytic, can even be potentially measured by psychometric tests. In these cases the constructs used are often contrived and overly approximated forms of it that have been dis-embedded from ordinary experience, are overly defined, are evaluated in terms of a single correct answer, and do not arouse any natural interest or motivation to the "solver." Practical and creative intelligence, on the other hand, are far more naturally occurring and represent what one *really* needs to know, allowing for true motivation for problem solving.[11]

Additionally, Sternberg emphasizes the cultural context for the conceptualization of intelligence, an aspect that he argues is virtually ignored by the psychometric approach. As he states, "[i]ntelligence is always *displayed* [italics in original] in a cultural context. The acontextual study of intelligence imposes a (usually western) investigator's view of the world on the rest of the world."[12] This concept is sensitive not only to differences between major cultures, for example, Western frames of thought versus Middle Eastern or Eastern frames of thought, but also to subcultures within major cultures such as black and Latino culture within an overarching American culture or Asian culture within an overarching immigrant culture.

As such, there are a number of factors that must be considered outside of natural inclination when determining the makeup of intelligence. As Sternberg suggests:

> In general, people of higher socioeconomic standing tend to have more opportunities and people of lower socioeconomic status have fewer. The economy or

political situation of the society can also be factors. Other variables that may affect such opportunities are education (especially literacy), political party, race, religion, and so forth. … Thus, how and how well an individual adapts to, shapes and selects environments must always be viewed in terms of the opportunities available to them.[13]

Sternberg's critique is directly applicable to the approach that American schools have been making in their attempts to evaluate and categorize students into various tracks and modalities through the use of standardized cognitive tests. While it may be popularly thought that since intelligence tests are "mathematical" and "scientifically validated," they are therefore objective and trustworthy; this idea has been both theoretically and empirically challenged, if not virtually debunked. As Hiser and Francis suggest:

> The question arising from these points is still, what do IQ tests measure? To suppose they are measuring "basal ability" in general would go against the point previously made that [innate abilities are] not directly accessible since physiological/biological factors seem to be mostly responsible for this attribute. To suggest that IQ tests are purely a measure of future success is also equally flawed. Indeed, much of the opprobrium related to IQ testing has risen from the misconception that such tests were supposed to give such information, and have been found to be inappropriate.[14]

Despite the quantitative analysis that can go into psychometrically evaluating a cognitive test, the test itself was always, and will always be, a product of the cultural context in which intelligence is conceptualized. The only means by which intelligence can become an actual utile concept that is informative in education is by eliminating the assumption that the Western (if not specifically American) approach is standard, and should be superimposed upon all explorations of intelligence. As Sternberg further explains:

> When cultural context is taken into account, (i) individuals are better recognized for and are better able to make use of their talents, (ii) schools teach and assess children better, and (iii) society uses rather than wastes the talents of its members. We can pretend to measure intelligence across cultures simply by translating western tests and giving them to individuals in a variety of cultures. But such measurement is only pretence. Individuals in other cultures often do not do well on our tests, nor would we do well on theirs. The processes of intelligence are universal, but their manifestations are not.[15]

With the notion of the unilateral approach to intelligence testing, especially those qualifiers of it based on psychometric tests, reflecting America's insistence on quantification and validation, it becomes clear that the advent of the intelligence test provided an instrument by which the elite could not only preserve their hegemony, but also validate it in the name of "science." This allowed further the gaining of "evidence" for their dominance as being the "natural order" of things, a notion that has been abused in multiple means of discrimination and exclusionary practices based on race, gender, ethnicity, or ability. As such, these notions are far more reflective of a cultural and political necessity than true science.

In effect, the concept of the quantification of intelligence can be easily reversed. Instead of America's lasting faith in quantitative test scores being used as evidence for the American culture's tacit insistence on white hegemony and the maintenance of class systems, it can just as easily be used to validate the questionable notion upon which America is built: the middle-class standard, and the use of dubious tests to validate the supremacy of the middle-class standard.

Therefore, the standardized test can serve two major functions in an assimilationist society. First, it can measure who, among the outsiders, have met middle-class standards, allowing for their acceptable inclusion and their use as proof that one can "overcome" social disadvantage. Second, it can serve as validation for the continuous exclusion of those who do not meet its standard by way of perceived cultural or individual deficiency.

It is this same concept of the "innate value" of the quantification of individuals' abilities that has guided the standards-based movements in education throughout history, and it is on the same basis of exclusion and expulsion that has solidified the value of middle-classism in schools.

There is, however, yet another fundamental mistake that has been perpetually present in discussions about intelligence, one that is the very same that Goddard originally made in his erroneous and decontextualized adaptation of the Binet-Simon test. That is, that these metrics were to be used in order to validate what one *can do*, and be seen as a generally static indicator of both capacity (in terms of aptitude) and worth (in terms of resources delivered) without attention paid to the extraneous factors that affect such a metric outside of the relatively narrow and statistically unfit conceptualization of socioeconomic status.[16]

In essence, these tests, as are the tests currently used to assess students' mastery of the curriculum, are less metric evaluations of cognitive or academic prowess than they are a tool of the legitimization of the social and cultural preoccupation with ranking, differentiating, and valuing people based on culturally perceived aspects of importance. In this sense standardized assessments legitimize nothing but the hegemonic culture's preoccupation with their own dominance, and their desperate grasp to any concept that can be used to validate it.

NOTES

1. Corwin Boake, "From the Binet-Simon to the Wechsler-Bellevue: Tracing the History of Intelligence Testing." *Journal of Clinical and Experimental Neuropsychology*, 24 no. 3, (2002): 383–405.

2. Ibid.

3. Stephen Jay Gould, *The Mismeasure of Man* (New York: W.W. Norton & Co., 1996), 21.

4. Spearman, 1927, as cited by Elizabeth Hiser and Carl Francis, "Intelligence: A Brief History." Journal of Inquiry and Research, 72, (2000).

5. Ulric Neisser et al. "Intelligence: Knowns and Unknowns." American Psychologist, 51 no. 2, (1996), 77–101.

6. Robert J. Gregory, *Psychological Testing: History, Principles, and Applications (6th ed.)* (New York: Allyn & Bacon, 2011).

7. Orlando Lourenco and Armanda Machado, "In Defense of Piaget's Theories: A Reply to 10 Common Criticisms." *Psychological Review,* 103 no. 1, (1997): 143–164.

8. Lev S. Vygotsky, "Interaction between learning and development." In M.Cole, V. John-Steiner, S. Scribner and E. Souberman (Eds.). *Mind in society: The development of higher psychological processes.* pp. 79–91. (Cambridge, MA: Harvard University Press, 1978).

9. Jennifer L. Nolen, "Multiple Intelligences in the Classroom." *Education,* 124 no. 1, (2003): 115–119.

10. Daniel Fasko, Jr., "An Analysis of Multiple Intelligences Theory and its Use with the Gifted and Talented." *Roeper Review*, 23 no. 3, (2001): 127–130.

11. Ibid.

12. Robert J. Sternberg and Elena L. Grigorenko, "Intelligence and Culture: How Culture Shapes What Intelligence Means, and the Implications for a Science of Well-Being." *Philosophical Transactions of the Royal Society of London*, 359, (2004), 1427.

13. Ibid.

14. Hiser and Francis, "Intelligence," 125.

15. Sternberg and Grigorenko, "Intelligence and Culture," 1433.

16. Ken Richardson, "What IQ Tests Test." Theory & Psychology, 12 no. 3, (2002): 283–314.

Chapter 11

Able Minds, Able Bodies

Ableism and the Public School

While the ideas of racism, classism, sexism, and ethnocentrism remain a focal point of critical discourse in contemporary scholarship on education, the perniciousness of ableism often remains elusive to mainstream conceptualizations of educational discrimination. Likely due to the presumed legitimacy of the medical model of disability in Western culture, or the idea that disability is an inherently negative attribute that must be overcome, or at least acceptably rehabilitated in order to be qualified for participation in mainstream society, ableism remains, in many cases, a legitimized form of discrimination. Rauscher and McClintock provide a comprehensive definition of ableism as

> a pervasive system of discrimination and exclusion that oppresses people who have mental, emotional and physical disabilities. ... Deeply rooted beliefs about health, productivity, beauty, and the value of human life, perpetuated by the public and private media, combine to create an environment that is often hostile to those whose physical, mental, cognitive, and sensory abilities ... fall out of scope of what is currently defined as socially acceptable.[1]

Douglas Baynton proffers an interesting perspective on the cultural permissiveness of ableism, especially as a defense against discrimination for other marginalized groups, namely racial and ethnic minorities as well as women. In his thesis, Baynton suggests that the permissiveness of discrimination based on disability plays out twofold. First, those who are doing the discriminating will justify the discrimination of other groups based on the presumption of disability (i.e., women and minority groups are inherently intellectually inferior). In response, those groups who are victims of the discrimination will retort by denying their inherent disability and proclaiming that they should not be treated as if they were disabled. This denial acts as an ironic device which argues against the discrimination based on gender, race, and ethnicity while legitimizing discrimination based on ability.[2]

The notion of ableism creates a similar contemporaneous narrative by suggesting that disabled people may, indeed, become figureheads of inspiration in a capitalistic society, but only by overcoming their disability and achieving seemingly unachievable feats. For example, a paraplegic who manages to climb a mountain, a woman with cerebral palsy who becomes a certified personal trainer, or a baseball pitcher who manages to be a successful player in the major leagues despite having only one hand. These individuals, often termed "supercrips," certainly do deserve recognition for their perseverance and their achievement.

However, the social roles they play, though involuntarily and likely even unwittingly, serve to propagate the narrative that disabled people are acceptable only when they overcome their disabling attribute. This leaves those individuals who either fail to overcome them, or choose to live with them, with not only less social and economic value, but also to be seen as lazy, apathetic, unmotivated, or worse, if receiving assistance, a socially and economically burdensome leach. These interpretations are akin to those leveled against minorities, especially black Americans and Hispanic immigrants, who are excoriated en masse on the same basis.

The result of this abelistic narrative is the maintenance of the "able-minded, able-bodied" hegemony whose deep influence is suffused across American culture and, inevitably if not resultantly, throughout educational culture and school infrastructure as well. However, ableism is propagated only by maintaining the centrality of the medical model of disability. That is, a disability is inherent to the individual, leaving the individual him/herself disabled regardless of location or environmental demand—hence, a *disabled person*.

One basis for a counter-narrative to the medical model of disability, however, is the biopsychosocial model, known more simply as the interactional model of disability, which places the source of disability not on the person, but on the interaction between the person and the environment, which is generally designed antagonistically to anyone outside of the "normative" body or cognitive type. From this perspective, disability is not to be seen as an inherent individual trait, but rather as a result of a discrepancy between environmental demands and individual physical or intellectual differences.[3]

Therefore, such issues with accessibility can be rectified by changing the environment to meet the needs of all individuals universally, rather than changing the individual to meet the demands of the environment. That is, a ramp can be used by someone who can walk *and* who requires a wheelchair, while stairs cannot; a verbal cue to cross an intersection when it is safe can be understood by those who can and cannot read or see, while a visual cue alone cannot.

The foundational nature of the difference between ableism and accommodation can be traced back in American society to colonial times, especially during the period in which most communities were sustenance based, and the pressures of production and provision were limited to one's own household and, perhaps, a small number of others in the surrounding area. During this period, individuals with various types of physical or intellectual differences were able to legitimately contribute to the community in various ways, be they adapted for their challenges, such as accepting less output from these workers or matched to their capabilities, such as allowing workers with challenges to complete tasks that did not interfere with their physical or mental difficulties. In either case, the individual was both included and valued for his or her contribution to the communal endeavor.

However, with the advent of the Industrial Revolution, when the focus of American productivity shifted from sustenance-based to export-based, the role of the disabled worker was critically compromised, especially considering the increasing presence of both technology such as machines that can complete tasks formerly carried out by a person, as well as the influx and increased availability of able-bodied immigrant workers, both of which provided faster, cheaper and more productive results of labor. As a result, many disabled workers found themselves unemployed, under-valued, and disregarded from society.

In an attempt to ameliorate the situation for individuals with physical disabilities, known then as "cripples," the government began to provide permits called "beggar's licenses," which allowed these individuals to panhandle, mostly in the swiftly developing urban centers, in order to make wages. Interestingly, the term "handicap," used often to describe people with disabilities in a general sense grew out of this phase in history based on the image of a beggar holding his "cap" in his "hand" (hand-in-cap—"handicap").[4]

With capitalism taking a stronghold on the American economy and the social notion of "rugged individualism" defining the prototypical capable American, the image of the "cripple" came to represent its antithesis to not only the American culture, but the quintessential American man.

Similarly, the increasing need for "cripples" to beg in order to make wages created a problem in nascent urban areas, which ultimately stymied the willingness for businesses to operate and people to congregate about these centers as a result of the ever-growing presence of this nuisance group. The government was then compelled to search for a solution to the emerging "cripple problem," a problem the government, itself, created by disallowing any other form of gainful employment aside from begging.[5]

One of the first attempts at containing the influx of crippled beggars was the establishment of the New York Hospital for the Crippled and Ruptured in the early 1900s. While clearly serving the main purpose of providing a depot for the crippled vagrants who were seen as increasingly problematic to the functioning of the burgeoning new urban centers, James Knight, the director of the program, became legitimately interested in the idea of rehabilitation for individuals with physical disabilities. While Knight's view was clearly centered in the medical model of disability, other supporters of this type of school voiced contrary perspectives that would represent precursors to the interactional model that would be resonated a half-century later with the growing Disability Rights Movement.

One such individual was Douglas McMurtrie who claimed that "the greatest handicap is not a loss of limb or other disability but the weight of public opinion."[6] McMurtrie later became instrumental in the establishment of his own school, the Red Cross Institute for Crippled and Disabled Men, for which he garnered support and funding from the U.S. Surgeon General's office, establishing an early connection between governmental provisions for individuals with disabilities. According to McMurtrie, the goal of the institute was not only physical rehabilitation for the individual, but also a means of effecting social change regarding public opinion of individuals with physical disabilities, in that the goal was to

> create an enlightened public opinion towards the physically handicapped, so that they will be regarded from the standpoint of their capabilities rather than their disabilities ... [which was] undoubtedly the most important phase of the whole question.[7]

Despite the initial intention of rehabilitation, however, larger populations of residents (patients) and dwindling staff-to-patient ratios resulted in the need for larger and often less regulated facilities. Based on this lack of attention and unmet need in adequate supervision, the conditions within these hospital-schools became increasingly more squalid, with many becoming abject to the point of blatant abuse and neglect. This neglect came often in the name of "science," such as doctors experimenting with early forms of prosthesis using unsanitary materials such as piano strings, nails, and screws.[8]

The handling of individuals with intellectual and developmental disabilities in America was to follow a similar trajectory of severe devaluation. While people with intellectual and developmental disabilities, known throughout history by many monikers including the feeble-minded, dim-wits, simpletons, and moron/idiot/imbecile (an example of early clinical designation), were ever seen as pitiable, history reveals a consequential difference between the result of such pity that began as charitableness and transformed into social and moral devaluation and degradation.

In the early 19th century the dominant Christian perspective maintained the notion that that those simple children (known in the children's narrative as "simple Simons") were to be regarded with compassion and helped, as they were to be perceived as harmless, innocent, eternal children. Tales such as "Mr. Feeble Mind" by John Bunyan assisted in cultivating this mentality. However, with the growing significance of the Industrial Revolution and the increasing importance of capitalistic function, individual capability, and American prosperity, any form of "misfit" became vilified, if not criminalized.[9]

Adding to this nascent ableist mentality was the increasing popularity of William Graham Sumner's concept of "social Darwinism" and Sir Francis Galton's theory of eugenics, or the essentiality of "good breeding" in a prosperous society. As these perspectives grew in popularity, the notion of institutionalization for individuals with intellectual and developmental disabilities, as well as those with physical disabilities, became well grounded in the American response to this seemingly growing population. By the middle of the 20th century institutionalization became the most available and preferred option for the medical community. Parents who had children with virtually any form of disability pressured to commit them to an institution and "forget about them."[10]

As public schools became increasingly more accessible to greater numbers of students, its role as "sieve" and its sorting of less responsive individuals, soon to be known as "slow and backward children" or "laggards" also grew more significant. According to J.E. Wallace Wallin:

> In the regular grades the feeble-minded and subnormal represent, as it were, an unassimilated accumulation of human clinkers, ballast, drift wood, or derelicts which seriously retards the rate of progress of the entire class and which often constitutes a positive irritant to the teacher and other pupils.[11]

Similarly, a hitherto anonymous official from a Providence, Rhode Island, school suggested:

> Our teachers in the regular school found so much relief when disorderly pupils were transferred to the disciplinary schools, that they were not slow to request the removal of the backward or mentally deficient children, who were receiving comparatively little benefit in their schools, to the same school for special instruction.[12]

While the initial intent of these "special schools" were similar to those of the hospital-schools for the physically disabled in that they were to provide rehabilitation followed by reintroduction to mainstream society, the ableist mentality propagated by Galton and Sumner took stronghold in the highly individualistic and capitalistic society, and transformed the idea of the alternative and rehabilitative school into the notorious institution. In time these institutions became the depot for any individual who was seen as a "misfit" for any reason, functioning entirely as a prison than as a place of rehabilitation.

Similarly to the hospital-schools, with America's increasing involvement in World War II, the population of institutions burgeoned unprecedentedly, increasing both the overall number of residents per school as well as the diminution of staff members. Additionally, this general burgeoning led to the institutionalization of an increasing number of children 5 years old and under whom, by the middle of the century, represented nearly one-third of institutionalized residents.[13]

The tension between those who advocated to contain individuals who were regarded as subnormal, especially in ways that were physically obvious and those who were to support their inclusion in society was to become a common one in American social discourse for the remainder of the 20th century and into the 21st century. The question as to whether individuals who posed physical and mental challenges should become a part of society only after, and contingent on, their rehabilitation and how they should be handled in the absence of sufficient rehabilitation formed the basis of what was to become the Disability Rights Movement.

In the 1950s, though slow to gain fervor, many parents of children with both physical and intellectual disabilities began to oppose the notion that their children were "broken" and should be discarded. Banding together by forming a number of advocacy groups including the National Association for Retarded Children (now known as AHRC or ARC), United Cerebral Palsy, March of Dimes, and the National Society for Crippled Children, later known as Easter Seals, parents began to compel greater society to regard children with disabilities as equally valuable to those without.[14]

In the early 1960s, President John F. Kennedy, largely as a result of his experience with his sister Rosemary, who had an intellectual disability, also began to push for the recognition of the rights of people with disabilities. As he famously stated:

> The manner in which our Nation cares for its citizens and conserves its manpower resources is more than an index to its concern for the less fortunate. It is a key to its future. Both wisdom and humanity dictate a deep interest in the physically handicapped, the mentally ill, and the mentally retarded. Yet although considerable progress in the treatment of physical handicaps, although we have attacked on a broad front the problems of mental illness, although we have made great strides in the battle against disease, we as a Nation have far too long postponed an intensive search for solutions to the problem of the mentally retarded. This failure should be corrected.[15]

The interest in the rights of individuals with disabilities remained and reached a critical mass in the early 1970s with two landmark cases: *Pennsylvania Association for Retarded Citizens (PARC) v. Commonwealth of Pennsylvania* and *Mills v. Board of Education of Washington, D.C.* Both cases argued against the discrimination and school refusal of children with disabilities. Resultantly, these cases were instrumental in leading to the first comprehensive antidiscrimination law for students with disabilities, the Education for all Handicapped Children Act (EHA), reauthorized and renamed in 1990 as the Individuals with Disabilities Education Act (IDEA), the cornerstone of special education practice in contemporary American schools.

However, while legislative efforts have clearly been made to compel the inclusion of individuals with disabilities into more mainstream educational environments, a similar fate to that of *Brown v. Board of Education* and the Civil Rights Act of 1965 has been observed. Though laws may compel compliance in certain perspectives, they cannot compel a change in public perception or culture, nor can they prevent the involved parties in discovering and capitalizing on loopholes in order to maintain the typical discriminatory ways of operating. This permissibility of loopholing by social institutions, especially schools, allowed society to continue to operate under a deep modality of ableism while still technically remaining within the boundaries of the law.

Despite the new legislative precedent prohibiting a school district to deny a child with a disability an education, the nature of *where* such an education is to be provided became pressing. The main criteria, as put forth by IDEA, for public school districts to determine the setting of education for students with disabilities was that of "least restrictive environment" (LRE). A likely intentionally vague term, the nature of "restrictiveness" was, and continues to be, one of the most contentious issues in education, especially regarding the appropriateness of educational placement for students with disabilities.

Using the concept of LRE, many districts continued to place students with disabilities either in external school placements (like alternative preschools, elementary schools, or secondary schools designed specifically for students with disabilities) that operated outside of the public school environment or within confined school spaces (such as placing students' self-contained classrooms housed in the physical plant of the public school building but having little, if any, interaction with the mainstream student body). These "alternative" placements are often justified using the claim of the districts' inability to provide the necessary supports for students with disabilities in general education environments.[16]

Within this practice, then, the only opportunity for a student with a disability to gain access to a mainstream environment is to "overcome" their disabilities (essentially, be less disabled) and earn their way into the general education environment. This perspective is set squarely within the ableist perspective. As Hehir suggests, "… given a human-made world designed with the nondisabled in mind, children with disabilities [only] gain an advantage if they can perform like their nondisabled peers."[17]

There are two main problems with this approach. First, when children are identified, often from the time they are very young, as disabled, they receive the message, almost continuously, that they cannot do things the way they are supposed to. As Hehir further suggests:

> Ableist assumptions become dysfunctional when the education and development services provided to disabled children focus on their disability to the exclusion of all else. From an early age, many people with disabilities encounter the view that disability is negative and tragic and that "overcoming" disability is the only valued result.[18]

Second, and perhaps more importantly, to require an individual to "overcome" something before they are granted access to an entity that is rightfully theirs (such as public schooling with their peers) is a violation of both civil rights and social justice. In the same vein that denying schooling to a black child who is underperforming due to "cultural deprivation" is unjustified, so is denying schooling to a child with a disability who is not "able-bodied" or "able-minded." Schooling is not simply for those who can engage in it "as planned," but is a right for all children in America regardless of their ability to meet the arbitrary ableist, racist, classist, sexist, and ethnocentrist standards of the American public school.

NOTES

1. Laura Rauscher and Mary J. McClintock. (1996). Ableism curriculum design. In M. Adams, L.A. Bell, and P. Griffen (Eds.) Teaching for Diversity and Social Justice (pp. 198–231). New York: Routledge. p. 198.

2. Douglas Baynton, "Disability and the Justification of Inequality in American History." *Mental Retardation*, 40 no. 1, (2002): 51–55.

3. Eric Shyman, *Beyond Equality in the American Classroom: The Case for Inclusive Education* (Lanham, MD: Lexington Books, 2013).

4. James A Henretta, "Families and Farms: Mentalité in Pre-Industrial America." *The William & James Quarterly*, 35 no. 1, (1980): 3–32.

5. Shyman, *Beyond Equality*.

6. Douglas McMurtrie, as cited by Brad Byrom, "A Pupil and a Patient" in Longmore, Paul K. and Lauri Umanski. *The New Disability History: American Perspectives* (New York: NYU Press, 2001), 138.

7. Ibid., 144.

8. Shyman, *Beyond Equality*.

9. James W. Trent, *Inventing the Feeble Mind: A History of Mental Retardation in the United States*. Los Angeles: University of California Press, 1995.

10. Down Syndrome Human and Civil Rights Timeline. Retrieved from http://www.globaldownsyndrome.org/about-down-syndrome/history-of-down-syndrome/down-syndrome-human-and-civil-rights-timeline/.

11. J.E. Wallace Wallin, *The Education of Handicapped Children* (New York: Houghton Mifflin, 1924), 92–93.

12. Trent, *Inventing the Feeble Mind*, 149.

13. Shyman. *Beyond Equality*.

14. Ibid.

15. Retrieved from http://www/mndcc.org/parallels2/pdf/60s/62/62-sallinger-pr.pdf.

16. Naomi Zigmond, "Where Should Students with Disabilities Receive Special Education Services?" *The Journal of Special Education*, 37 no. 3, (2003): 193–199.

17. Thomas Hehir, "Eliminating ableism in education." *Harvard Educational Review,* 72, (2002): 1–32.

18. Thomas Hehir, "Confronting Ableism." *Educational Leadership*, 64 no. 5, (2007): 8–14.

Chapter 12

Segregation's New Stripes

Race, Language, and Special Education

While it has been well established that the general public school system has deep roots in racial and ethnic segregation and has, in many ways, perpetuated the dominant narratives within its explicit and tacit curricula, there is, simultaneously, a far less discussed but equally as pernicious discriminatory practice regularly at work in schools: segregation within the special education system. The disproportionality of black students as well as ethnically and linguistically diverse students, namely nonnative English-speaking Hispanic children, has been historically documented for at least three decades.

However, this overrepresentation in special needs areas and underrepresentation in gifted and talented areas remain ironic at their core. As Sullivan states:

> For a field built on the principle of fairness, formed in the wake of Brown v. Board of Education, and grounded in the rhetoric of the civil rights movement, ongoing disproportionality [of black and Hispanic students in special education] strongly indicates systemic problems of inequity, prejudice, and marginalization within the education system.[1]

Indeed, this truth represents a dire hypocrisy, but also signifies the deep-seated nature of the systemic processes of American schooling that hold race and ethnicity at a practical core. Though, the formal special education system proceeded even the most conservative estimates of the establishment of the public schooling system by at least three-quarters of a century, it has managed to perpetuate, seemingly inherently, the very basis of its segregated practices based on racial and ethnic boundaries.

It is important to clarify what is meant by the term "disproportionality" as it relates to representation in special education. While there are a number of

107

ways in which researchers measure disproportionality, the general denotation of the term suggests representation in special education as a ratio to the group's representation among the total population. Therefore, a disproportionality does not necessarily indicate that there are *more kids* of a certain group in special education, but rather that there is a higher percentage of students in relation to their total representation in the population. For example, if there is a representation of 33 percent of black children in a particular school system's special education program, but only a 17 percent representation of black children across the same school system's population, disproportionality is indicated.[2]

By far, the research investigating disproportionality in special education preponderantly handles issues of race. Evidence of segregated practices based on race in special education date back as far as 1968, before formal special education legislation, in the form of PL 94-142, was even established. A report released at the time declared that upwards of 60–80 percent of students taught in what was then known as "mentally retarded" classrooms were from "low status backgrounds," specifically black, Mexican, American Indian, and Puerto Rican.[3] Similar statistics continued through the 1980s, and have remained consistent over time, even to the present day.[4]

Disproportionate representations in special education as a whole tell only a fraction of the story, however. There is also clear evidence that black children have a much higher likelihood of being diagnosed and educationally classified in particular categories of disabilities. Educational classifications such as mental retardation and emotional disturbance are applied to black children in a disproportionately large ratio, while they are less likely to be classified in others, particularly specific learning disabilities and speech-language impairments.

These "risk ratios" can be as much as triple for black children than they are for other ethnicities comparatively, especially white children.[5,6] Interestingly, these areas of overrepresentation also implicate disabilities for which students are most likely to be placed in external school placements or self-contained classrooms,[7] increasing the chance that segregated settings be maintained based both on race as well as disability classification.[8,9]

Though the research is far less substantial, there is also an emerging evidence-basis for the overrepresentation of English Language Learners (ELL), mainly of Hispanic origin, in the special education system. Part of the reason for such a dearth of research is a more distinct lack of interest in examining the experience of immigrant children by the general research community. However, a more empirically based problem is both the staggered presence of Hispanic communities in the United States, as well as the highly transitory nature of many Hispanic inhabitants, disallowing for truly consistent or reliable data upon which conclusions can be made. Further, the lack of systematic monitoring systems at the local school district levels for ELL students contributes to the dearth of information, making analysis nearly impossible.

Despite these challenges, however, data analyzed for states with a more significant Hispanic population, such as California, Texas, and Florida, do affirm overrepresentation in special education.[10] Some analysts suggest that there is as high as a 17 percent representation of ELL children in special education,[11] while some estimates are slightly more conservative at roughly 14 percent or less.[12] Despite the range, however, it appears to be clear that the generally accepted definition of disproportionality would still apply, even in the case of more conservative estimates, as ELL students comprise a relatively low proportion of the general population nationally.

Such an analysis, however, remains entirely encyclopedic without an investigation into the potential causes of such practices. While there are no definitive indices of how such a discriminatory system came into being, there are a number of hypotheses that are supported by emerging research. These hypotheses include psychometric test bias, teacher perspectives and referral bias, teacher efficacy, and general cultural perceptions of black and nonnative Hispanic children, especially as it relates to power and hegemony.

Issues surrounding psychometric tests are abounding and ever-present in education, as evidenced earlier. The educational system's overreliance on these vastly imperfect, if at all meaningful, tests have allowed for the justification of segregation and exclusionary practices in multiple ways. The area of racial and ethnic discrimination in special education is no different. Indeed, the long-standing notion that psychometric tests, especially those that are widely available, represent culturally rooted notions of intelligence more than anything has been demonstrated in a variety of ways and remains applicable in the special education context. As such, these same deep-seated issues play a significant role in cultural disproportionality.

Despite the defense of such tests being validated using normative data, such normative data are often comprised of un-diverse samples reflecting the same disproportionality, that is, a dire lack of racial, ethnic, and socioeconomic diversity in the normative samples themselves.[13,14] Indeed, black children typically score lower on standardized IQ tests not as a result of an "inherently" lower cognitive capacity, but more likely as a result of schooling and community experience lacking in exposure to and emphasis on the very environmental and culturally relevant elements that such psychometric tests assess.[15] The results of these testing protocols themselves represent one of the more obvious vicious circles in the educational system.

One clear ramification of such testing bias is the likelihood of black children being diagnosed as having "mental retardation" (or the contemporary term "intellectual disability" in many states) as opposed to specific learning disabilities, which can only be assigned in the absence of such factors as intellectual disability and, more importantly challenged or disadvantaged environments, in which many black children do, indeed, reside. In this sense, the categorical criteria alone all but preclude many black children from receiving SLD classifications as opposed to other, less diagnostically exclusionary categories such as Intellectual Disability/Mental Retardation or Emotional-Behavioral Disturbance. Indeed, it is the outcome of such psychometric tests that virtually dictate the outcomes of such a classification system.

The issue of psychometric tests affects ELLs as well. Since the 1980s, many ELL children, upon arriving in schools, were given psychometric evaluations in English as opposed to their native language, a practice that, though much less common, still exists in many areas. Deepening this problem, many practitioners who are not well-trained in the area of evaluating nonnative speakers of English are unable to distinguish between emergent English proficiency and a language disability, leading to frequent conflation between language acquisition and learning challenges. This problem becomes even more prominent when tests that rely heavily on language are used.[16]

Teacher-based issues also contribute significantly to racial and ethnic disproportionality in special education. Aspects such as referral bias among teachers as well as teacher sense of efficacy for teaching culturally and linguistically diverse students have been supported by emerging evidence, indicating the increasing exigency to address them.[17]

Much research indicates that teachers as well as administrators have a higher likelihood of referring black and Hispanic children for special education than they do white children.[18,19] Indices of over-referral are multifaceted, but tend to point toward teacher-related aspects such as lack of attention given to pre-referral strategies, a push toward testing, and a general lack of knowledge regarding language issues.[20]

Teacher sense of efficacy with specific regard to culturally or linguistically diverse students has also been shown to be a significant issue in the disproportionality. Sense of efficacy, or a teacher's belief that he or she is capable of executing instruction with meaningful results, has a strong presence in the larger teacher quality literature, and it is therefore unsurprising that it would relate to a specific population as well.[21]

Given the challenges that a diverse population would pose to a teacher, it is logical that teachers with a higher sense of efficacy would be more successful with culturally and linguistically diverse students. Quite interestingly, one study found that the most significant correlation with both sense of efficacy as well as student outcome was the teacher ability to speak the students' native language. This finding, though seminal, suggests that a culturally responsive approach may be more likely to positively affect diverse students' schooling experience. Some research indicates similar findings for black children who are taught by those that are more familiar with their particular culture, especially other black teachers.[22]

Perhaps the most relevant indicator, however, is the one that is most deeply present in American society and one that has been addressed repeatedly in the current work: the dominant cultural narratives that are maintained and pervaded through institutions such as public schooling. These narratives, as expressed, contain often tacit but deeply rooted messages about the quality and nature of "others," that is, those who are not part of the hegemonic group. Embedded in these narratives are descriptive validations of pervasive cultural practices that maintain the oppression and the cultural illegitimacy of the "other" and permit the systematic nature of discriminatory practices to continue.

This idea can be conceptualized as "cultural reproduction" and has been shown to be both well documented and nearly ubiquitous.[23] An important facet of cultural reproduction is its very tacit nature. That is, people who function in a given society unconsciously yet habitually behave in ways that reproduce cultural narratives at both the personal and institutional level as a result of their oft-reinforced cultural preconceptions. Such behaviors include low expectations of academic achievement among culturally and linguistically diverse students, higher expectation and implementation of disciplinary practices, and a general notion of containment rather than mobility, as indicated by the higher proportion of minorities who are relegated to restrictive educational placements.

Essentially, it is the imperious role of hegemony that underscores all of the above-mentioned issues from the seemingly practical and clinically driven, such as diagnostic and classification protocols, to the very personally driven, such as teacher referral behavior and sense of efficacy. Hegemony, as defined by McLaren, is

> the maintenance of the domination not by sheer exercise of force but primarily through consensual social practices, social forms, and social structures produced in specific sites such as the church, the state, the school, the mass media, the political system, and the family.[24]

As a result, certain preconceptions involving race, even among those who do not see themselves as racist, per se, act socially and politically in such ways that reinforce these cultural notions and maintain their social outplay.

Perhaps the clearest way to describe both the tacit and pervasive nature of this process is through what Eddie S. Glaude Jr. refers to as "racial habits." According to Glaude:

> Racial habits don't come out just in interactions between white people and black people. We're wrong when we think the problem of racial inequality rests

simply with discrimination, whether by overt racists or people unconsciously enacting racial habits. This approach locates the problem elsewhere—with the bad people over there, safely securing most of us from the idea that our actions and snap judgments contribute, in any way, to racial inequality. Thinking in this way denies that the problem may be with the way we *all* [emphasis in original] live our lives, even in arenas that seem to have nothing to do with race. Something much more banal and pernicious is definitely at work.[25]

In this Glaude reminds us that racism or ethnocentrism is not simply an *act* of hatred or bigotry or discrimination against another. Rather, it is a systemic process that involves all individuals in any institution of American society. Even when such acts are unintentional, if they serve to propagate the nefarious workings of cultural reproduction, solidifying the ever damning presumptions of race and ethnicity in practice, we are, indeed, contributing to the problem.

NOTES

1. Amanda Sullivan, "Disproportionality in Special Education Identification and Placement of English Language Learners." *Exceptional Children,* 77 no. 3, (2011): 317–334.

2. Alfredo J. Artiles et al., "Overidentification of Students of Color in Special Education: A Critical Overview." *Multicultural Perspectives,* 4 no. 1, (2002): 3–10.

3. Ibid.

4. Russell Skiba, "Achieving Equity in Special Education: History, Status, and Current Challenges." *Exceptional Children,* 74 no. 3, (2008): 264–288.

5. Ibid.

6. J.K. Klinginger et al., "Addressing the Disproportionate Representation of Culturally and Linguistically Diverse Students in Special Education through Culturally Responsive Educational Systems." *Education Policy Analysis Archives,* 13 no. 38, (2005). Retrieved from http://epaa.asu.edu/epaa/v13m38.

7. Sullivan, "Disproportionality in Special Education."

8. Skiba et al., "Achieving Equity in Special Education."

9. Tamela McNulty Eitle, "Special Education or Racial Segregation: Understanding Variation in the Representation of Black Students in Educable Mentally Handicapped Programs." *The Sociological Quarterly,* 43 no. 4, (2002): 575–605.

10. Alfredo J. Artiles et al., "Within-Group Diversity in Minority Disproportionate Representation: English Language Learners in Urban School Districts." *Exceptional Children,* 71 no. 2, (2005): 283–300.

11. Sullivan, "Disproportionality in Special Education."

12. Klingenger et al., "Addressing Disproportionate Representation."

13. Ann B. Shuttleworth-Edwards, Ryan D. Kemp, Annegret L. Rust et al., "Cross-cultural Effects on IQ Test Performance: A Review and Preliminary Normative Indications on the WAIS-III Test Performance." *Journal of Clinical and Experimental Neuropsychology,* 26 no. 7, (2004): 903–920.

14. Monica Roselli and Alfredo Ardila, "The Impact of Culture and Education on Non-Verbal Neuropsychological Measurements: A Critical Review." *Brain and Cognition,* 52, (2003): 326–333.

15. Beth Harry and Janette Klingner, "Discarding the Deficit Model." *Educational Leadership,* 64 no. 5, (2007): 16–21.

16. Sullivan, "Disproportionality in Special Education."

17. Artiles et al., "Overidentification."

18. Russell Skiba et al., "The Context of Minority Disproportionality."

19. Todd A. Gravois and Sylvia A. Rosenfield, "Impact of Instructional Consultation Teams on the Disproportionate Referral and Placement of Minority Students in Special Education." *Remedial and Special Education,* 27 no. 1, (2006): 42–52.

20. Janette Klinginger and Beth Harry, "The Special Education Referral and Decision-Making Process for English Language Learners: Child Study Team Meetings and Staffings." *Teachers College Record, 108,* (2006): 2247–2281.

21. Oneyda M. Paneque and Patricia M. Barbetta, "A Study of Teacher Efficacy of Special Education Teachers of English Language Learners with Disabilities." *Bilingual Research Journal,* 30 no. 1, (2006): 171–193.

22. Carolyn M. Tucker et al., "Promoting Teacher Efficacy for Working with Culturally Diverse Students." *Preventing School Failure,* 50 no. 1, (2005): 29–34.

23. Skiba et al., "Context."

24. McLaren, as cited by Klingner, "Special Education Referral Process."

25. Eddie S. Glaude, Jr., *Democracy in Black: How Race Still Enslaves the American Soul.* (New York: Crown Publishers, 2015).

Chapter 13

You're an American Now

Assimilation or Elimination for the Non-American

Immigration has ever been a controversial matter in America. While ironic in some ways, being that all Americans, regardless of how far back their familial history in the country reaches, at some point descend from an immigrant family, the complex entanglement with the availability of perceived limited resources and political processes makes immigration an exceedingly fervent issue. At the heart of the immigration issue, however, is likely less of a discussion of immigration in general and more of a discussion about *who* should be permitted to immigrate to, enter, and stay in America. That is, who is desirable and undesirable, or deserving or undeserving at access to resources in a seemingly prosperous country?

Starting in 1885, a so-called new immigration began, characterized by many opponents as the replacement of "older sources" of immigration, particularly the "civilized" Western European countries such as England and France, with the "less civilized" Eastern European countries such as Poland, Czechoslovakia, Yugoslavia, and parts of Russia. This concern is expressed by Hoyt (1916):

> The consensus of opinion seems to be that this new immigration is far less desirable than the old, because of its lower standards of living, industrial backwardness, lack of sympathy with our type of institutions, and its marked differences from our predominant stock in religion, race, literacy, and industrial training. ...
> With the weakening of our capacity to provide for more immigrants, the people from the south and east of Europe have crowded to our shores in ever-increasing throngs; they have filled our cities with the babel of foreign tongues, and by their very numbers alone have added confusion and discord to our national councils.[1]

This trend of evaluating which immigrants are and are not desirable continues in American society. The backlash against Eastern and Southern

Europeans subsided, mainly as a result of their ability, as a group, to largely establish themselves as economically contributive to American society. However, the more contemporary aversion appears to be against Mexican, Central American, and South American immigrants for largely the same reasons. Evidence of aversion to the Latino population in particular was apparent as early as the 1960s.

An exemplary display of this tension played out in Crystal City, Texas. Though a majority of the student body of Crystal City schools was Mexican, the white students remained socially dominant while the Eurocentric academic curriculum was maintained. The message of the expectation of assimilation strongly entrenched in the school's culture remained very clear despite the whites being a vast minority. However, in 1968, in response to growing unrest and feelings of exclusion by the Mexican-American population in Crystal City, students organized a boycott of the school and usurped control of its Board of Education.

Using their newfound power and decision latitude, the new Mexican-American Board members strongly infused the curriculum with Mexican culture and interpretations of history in an attempt to more fairly represent their version of the narrative, especially given the predominance of its members of the student body. Interestingly, while most of the white students and teachers egressed the Crystal City public school system in response to the new "pro-Mexican" agenda (as it was described by the defectors), nearly 170 Mexican students who had previously dropped out returned.

As Jose Angel Guttierez, the newly elected Mexican-American Board president, proclaimed, "We gave people pride. We showed people that community groups can organize and take power and determine their destiny ... that they are part of the movement."[2]

Legislation reflective of the increasing special needs of immigrant children began to take shape in the second half of the 20th century, with the most significant initial development being the Bilingual Act of 1968, which was later incorporated as Title VII of the Elementary and Secondary Education Act (ESEA). This act mandated supports for all children who had "limited English-speaking ability."

Though "bilingual" in title, this act did not clarify whether policies should be established to "transition" (a clear euphemism for "assimilate") children with limited English language or to allow for the maintenance of their native language for receiving instruction. The thrust was clarified a bit by the introduction of $68 million in federal funds to support the translation of educational materials into nearly 70 languages in 1974. However, these developments in no way put the controversial issue to rest.[3] This debate remains at the forefront of contemporary discussions of bilingual education and the role that language of instruction plays in a still deeply assimilationist system.

While it is inaccurate to claim that the Latino/a immigrants hold a monopoly on immigrant discrimination (indeed, contemporarily Middle Eastern immigrants, especially from particular countries such as Iran, Afghanistan, and Syria have been discriminated against and denied entrance), their experience is one of the most valid studies of the aversion to and backlash against immigrants with a strong will to maintain their own culture while also participating in American society. The Latino/a experience is also a telling study in the inability of certain ethnicities as a whole (barring exceptions to the rule) to adeptly ascend the "American social ladder" while other groups were able to despite their willingness to contribute to labor, strength in numbers, and strong sense of cultural as well as moral values.

While there are a number of potential explanations as to why Latino/a youth have been far less successful in the American public education system than other immigrant ethnicities such as Eastern Europeans and Asians, there appears to be a consensus that there is a systematic barrier to their success as a group.

One of the most widely cited explanations is that of the perpetual low-income status of many Latino families, which forces their habitation in underdeveloped communities with ill-equipped schools, a situation virtually identical to, as well as coinciding with, that of the black community. A significant simultaneous factor is the general pervasiveness of low expectations of many teachers in these neighborhood schools (and greater society) and social and cultural misunderstanding of Latino/a youth who are often perceived as subversive and culturally disengaged, especially if they are of an extroverted nature.[4]

Other explanations for the systematic exclusion of Latino/a youth and their families include a lack of understanding of the US school system and their subsequent rights within it, low parental involvement in the schools, likely at least in part due to the need to maintain multiple jobs for subsistence, lack of residential stability minimizing the cultivation and maintenance of functional and vested Latino communities, and minimal bilingual or special educational support in neighborhood schools that serve Latino/a youth despite a higher ratio of special education referral.[5]

The combination of the requirement of assimilation and, in many cases, egression from their cultural communities coupled with the desire to maintain their own culture and cultural history despite their new geographical residency creates a seemingly impenetrable social barrier for Latino/a youth. This bargain becomes reminiscent of that which is also required of the black community. That is, if one is to meet the middle-class standard for acceptability, one must also shed any remnants of their culture which act in opposition to it.

But how can the disparate social and cultural trajectories of different immigrant groups, especially in the area of education, be explained? Ogbu and Simons (1998) offer what they characterize as a cultural-ecological model to attempt such an explanation. This model is comprised of two parts: (1) the system, which is characterized by the way that minorities are treated or mistreated in terms of educational policy, pedagogy, and return for their investment in the traditional American schooling system (including higher education); and (2) community forces, which are affected by the way a minority group perceives and responds to aspects of the system, as well as interpret why *they* have become a part of a "minority," and all of its consequences, to begin with.[6]

Ogbu and Simons then relate the notion of *collective problems of minorities*, which are problems that appear to affect minorities across distinctions. Such distinctions include *instrumental discrimination*, such as employment and wage disparity; *relational discrimination*, including residential and social segregation; and *symbolic discrimination*, namely defamation and devaluation of minority culture and language. As a response, minorities often engage in *collective solutions*, such as the development of a survival or success narrative, a notion of group-wide struggle and solidarity, and adopt either an unapologetic cultural framework or an acceptance of "white ways," or fulfilling those expectations of the hegemonic culture.[7]

Finally, the model classifies minorities into three distinct categories: (1) autonomous, (2) voluntary (immigrant), and (3) nonvoluntary (nonimmigrant). Autonomous groups are generally groups that are small in number and intentionally and unapologetically collect under an identity, such as Jews, Mormons, or Amish. The difference between autonomous minorities and voluntary minorities, despite even potential immigrant status, is the relatively low level of systematic discrimination each faces (though it is reasonable to believe that the groups themselves, namely Jews, would categorically disagree with this characterization based on past instances of systematic discrimination in America).

Voluntary minorities include those individuals who have willingly moved to America. This is not to say that they left their native country without need or exigency, but rather that they chose America as their destination as opposed to another country that may have been equally accessible. Essentially, their arrival and residency in the United States was not forced upon them. While many of these groups could likely be characterized as systematically discriminated against during the early part of their immigration (from the late 1800s into the first quarter of the 1900s) such as Eastern and Southern Europeans as well as the Irish and Italians, this discrimination has almost entirely subsided, at least at the systematic level. However, other groups, such as Latino/a immigrants from Central and South America and, specifically, Mexico, do, indeed, still experience systematic discrimination.

Involuntary minorities are people who reside in America by virtue of conquest, colonization, or slavery, namely Native Americans and blacks. These groups were either forced to take residency (such as black slaves) or became controlled and displaced by the American government despite the indigenousness (such as Native Americans) against their will. Involuntary minorities are distinguished in American society by having both their presence (in terms of where they live) as well as their position (in terms of how they are treated) as imposed by the hegemonic American cultural, economic, and governmental system (e.g., government, social, and dominant cultural factors).[8]

These functions of greater society largely dictate the resulting processes and experiences of these individuals in schools, with those still vilified voluntary minorities (such as Mexicans, Central and South Americans, and select Middle Easterners) being accorded the same systematic discrimination as those involuntary minorities. Such functions have a deep impact on the framework for both educational policy and practice.

According to this framework, four factors result: (1) a frame for comparison between minority and nonminority schools (such as "white" schools in suburbia versus "black /Hispanic" schools in the inner city); (2) beliefs about the value of schooling itself (such as whether there will be a social return on the investment in schooling for minorities); (3) relational interpretations of schooling (such as students' level of trust and faith in school personnel); and (4) symbolic beliefs about schooling and curriculum (such as whether or not the curriculum accurately and fairly reflects cultural values, interpretations, and identity). Given that the framework for American public schooling is dictated by the middle-class ethos, the likelihood of any of these factors being favorable is greatly diminished.[9]

A similar model is suggested by Eduardo Bonilla-Silva, which he calls the emerging tri-racial system. This system, he argues, is already established in a number of Latin American and Caribbean nations. According to a tri-racial system, the white Eurocentric predominance in America is maintained, with these dominant whites comprising the top tier of the racial system.

However, as a response to the swiftly minimizing prominence of the white person in proportion to the general American population, the system is becoming buffered by an intermediary group known as "honorary whites." These "honorary whites," while not necessarily white in complexion, represent immigrant groups that are seen as wholly contributive to the capitalistic system in America (i.e., almost as useful and valuable as whites) such as Japanese Americans, Korean Americans, Chinese Americans, certain Middle Eastern Americans (especially non-Muslims or assimilated Muslims from countries such as Israel, Turkey, and those who identify as "Persians" rather than Iranians), light-skinned Latinos (namely Cubans), and a number of multiracial sects (so long as one of the races is white). These "honorary whites" have either matched or come close to matching the capitalistic contributive status of white Americans in both economic and cultural realms and have assimilated acceptably into American culture.

It is important to distinguish, however, that the "honorary whites" are primarily those who are native to America, even first-generational, rather than their immigrant ancestors. It is further important to distinguish that the subset of middle-class black Americans are not included in this stratum, according to Bonilla's model.[10]

At the bottom of the tri-racial system is the "collective black," comprised of new immigrants and minorities that are seen as noncontributive to, if not a burden on, the capitalistic system, most notably dark-skinned Latinos (including Mexican, Central American and Dominican), West Indian and African immigrants, reservation-bound Native Americans, and native and nonnative blacks (especially those from Haiti, Jamaica, or other Caribbean countries). These members of the social strata comprise the undesirable element to society for both natives and new "permissible" immigrants, and are the general receptors of systematic bigotry and oppression from both the "whites" and the "honorary whites." Indeed, it is important to note that some variability, such as the black and Latino middle class, and other "assimilated" members of the "collective black," exists, allowing for some of these individuals to attain acceptable status based on a middle-class standard.[11]

Part and parcel of the emerging tri-racial system, in addition to the infrastructural establishment of the "honorary white" stratum, is the notion of a "new racism" or "smiling discrimination," which denies the salience of race in institutions and decries those who propagate its significance while deep-seated systematic practices are not only maintained, but deepened.[12] This type of racism is apparent in the increasing prevalence of apartheid schools, racially stratified housing patterns, and disproportionality of racial makeups of "higher" social institutions such as businesses, universities, and government.

These socially relevant strata function at all levels of society and are reauthorized and recapitulated at the formative level of society: the schools. Deeply engrained in school functioning, from dominant curricula to disciplinary processes, is the Eurocentric, middle-class grounded, "whiteness" based propriety of society. It is to this dominant structure that the developing identities of students are perpetually compared. For those fitting within this culture, including those that Bonilla deems as "honorary whites," schools are validating institutions which consistently reinforce the cultural viability of the "in-group."

However, for those who do not fit, namely the "collective black," schools, serve as persistent reminders of one's illegitimacy and burden on the rest of a deserving society. These messages are delivered not only through Eurocentric curricula, pervasively low expectations, and bigoted disciplinary practices, but also through the physical structures of the schools themselves, which are often dilapidated, unaesthetic, and filled with disciplinary admonition such as metal detectors, police presence, and prison-like control practices mimicking penitentiaries.

Within this deep and somewhat tacit social message is carried a more obvious one—obvious at least to those who are destined to receive it: you are not knowledge holders or creators; rather you are simply in school to receive the curriculum that will reinforce your inferiority and all but solidify your subordinate destiny.[13] These beliefs are cyclical and self-fulfilling, permeating all of society and influencing all social processes from religion to politics to legislation and educational reform. They are, therefore, seemingly indefatigable, leaving the victims of it as oppressed as they have ever been—and this is, indeed, the intention.

NOTES

1. Homer Hoyt, "The Relation of a Literacy Test to a Constructive Immigration Problem." *Journal of Political Economy,* 24 no. 5, (1916), 447.

2. Jose Angel Guttierez as cited by Ravitch, *The Troubled Crusade,* 157.

3. Ibid.

4. Gilberto Q. Conchas, "Structuring Failure and Success: Understanding the Variability in Latino School Engagement." *Harvard Educational Review,* 71 no. 3, (2001): 475.

5. Stephanie A. Bohon, Heather Macpherson, and Jorge H. Atiles, "Educational Barriers for New Latinos in Georgia." *Journal of Latinos and Education,* 4 no. 1, (2005): 43–58.

6. John U. Ogbu and Herbert D. Simons, "Voluntary and Involuntary Minorities: A Cultural-Ecological Theory of School Performance with Some Implications for Education." *Anthropology & Education Quarterly,* 29 no. 2, (1998): 55–188.

7. Ibid.

8. Ibid.

9. Ibid.

10. Eduardo Bonilla-Silva, "We are All Americans!: The Latin Americanization of Racial Stratification in the USA." *Race & Society,* 5, (2002): 3–16.

11. Ibid.

12. Eduardo Bonilla-Silva, *White Supremacy and Racism in the Post-Civil Rights Era.* Lynne Rienner Publishers: Boulder, CO, 2001.

13. Dolores Delgado Bernal, "Critical Race Theory, Latino Critical Theory, and Critical Raced-Gendered Epistemologies." Qualitative Inquiry, 8 no. 1, (2002), 105–126.

Chapter 14

It's a Man's World

Schooling and the Gender Gap

The notions of inequality are well established in the American social narrative, with a number of marginalized groups coming to the forefront. However, when it comes to discussions about schooling, the gender issue remains somewhat underrepresented in contemporary discourse outside of a relatively specialized field of academic study, namely in the area of social psychology and the ever-developing realm of Women's or Feminist studies. As Sadker and Sadker suggest:

> Mention educational inequality and, for most people, race comes to mind: black children walking down a dusty road to a dilapidated school while a bright yellow bus with white children passes them by; or an urban ghetto school with iron bards protecting already broken windows, a building ravaged by poverty and time. While the record of racial injustice is at the forefront of our national conscience, history books still do not tell the story of profound sexism at school. Few people realize that today's girls continue a three-hundred-year-old struggle for full participation in America's educational system.[1]

This deep system of exclusion remains far more tacit than those of other institutional forms. While recent history does not tell of a time where girls were deliberately excluded from schools, perhaps with the exceptional and somewhat different context of religious-based "girls' schools," the same Eurocentric curriculum that is used to maintain the subjugation of black children and immigrant children draws upon its "male" influence in order to also oppress girls and young women. The messages within the widely used textbooks were clear and consistent. The tales told were of the founding *fathers* and *male* inventors, war heroes and scientists, all of whom set the country on its positive course toward American supremacy.

123

There were, indeed gratuitous insertions of women periodically, and these insertions came only as a result of intense feminist advocacy, including the ever important stories of Marie Curie, Susan B. Anthony, and the general "woman" effort during the war such as the now mythologized "Rosie the Riveter." But these tales were relegated to supporting roles at best, and in many ways continue to be. As Sadker and Sadker further suggest:

> When girls do not see themselves in the pages of textbooks, when teachers do not point out or confront the omissions, our daughters learn that to be female is to be an absent partner in the development of our nation. And when teachers add their stereotypes to the curriculum bias in books, the message becomes even more damaging.[2]

Despite the lack of overt discrimination against girls and young women in recent history, early American history does, indeed, reveal a time when young girls were excluded. As early American schools tended to follow the European tradition, girls and young women were explicitly barred from attendance. Because girls and women were generally viewed as a morally and mentally inferior gender, the need or purpose of schooling for women was dismissed. Indeed, this sentiment was made clear even in the pro-education musings of Thomas Jefferson.

Women, at this time, were seen as serving domestic roles only: child rearing, housekeeping, and socializing to keep oneself "busy" and serve the husband and father. As Jefferson suggests:

> But our good ladies, I trust, have been too wise to wrinkle their foreheads with politics. They are contented to soothe [and] calm the minds of their husbands returning ruffled from political debate. They have the good sense to value domestic happiness above all other, and the art to cultivate it beyond all others.[3]

In some schools, girls were given one hour per day of schooling, but only after the boys were dismissed. In other schools, there were brief periods, both before and after the school day for boys, during which girls were provided an opportunity for education in exchange for an exorbitant fee. Though clearly unfair and reflective of the deeply misogynistic ways of the early American society, the notion of schooling girls began to be established from these seminal practices.

By the 1800s the establishment of girls' schools began to increase, such as the Young Ladies Academy in Philadelphia, established by the noted colonial educationist Dr. Benjamin Rush, and the Troy Seminary in New York. Though all of these new schools were generally couched within the terms of a maternal training ground, that is, places in which young women would learn to be good mothers and wives, far from the spirit of justice envisioned by the later feminist movement. By the end of the first quarter of the 19th century there was popular demand for equal schooling for girls, leading to the establishment of a regular girls' high school in Boston in 1820, and this trend followed nationwide.[4]

This brand of advocacy led to the wider spread establishment of girls' and boys' schools, largely kept separate from one another either by using separate buildings or, in the case of smaller towns, separate entrances to the same buildings. With more vocal advocates of coeducational schooling, or the housing and instruction of boys and girls in the same classrooms, such coeducational practices became a commonality of schooling in America's secondary schools in the 20th century.

The latter part of the 20th century also saw some political attention to the treatment of girls and young women, including Title IX, passed in 1972, which barred gender bias in school provisions such as athletics, counseling, admissions, and medical services, and the Women's Educational Equity Act in 1974, which was a compliance-based action associated with Title IX.[5]

The issue of gender inequality in American public schooling reaches deeper than an absent history or representation in the curriculum, however. Increasing research appears to demonstrate that the experience of girls and young women in schools as compared to that of boys are contributive, if not directly reinforcing, of the oppressive state of women in post-school society. It is important to note, though, that such research findings are inconsistent, and research citing contradictory findings can also be cited.[6] As Halpern and colleagues suggest:

> Opponents of the idea that biology has contributed even a small part to male and female differences are quick to label biological explanations as sexist … [though] biological hypotheses are not necessarily sexist. There does not have to be a "smarter sex" with a "better biology" to conclude that there are biological origins to any cognitive ability.[7]

There does, however, appear to be validity to the social and environmental influences of gender inequality in the classroom. These differences are often expressed in the form of teachers favoring boys in terms of attention, participation, and academic support.[8,9] Much of this research suggests that the relationship between the teacher and the student, especially in the formative developmental periods such as pre-kindergarten and kindergarten, are both essential to and predictive of academic achievement in subsequent grades.

As such, if there are gender differences between the teacher-student socialization dynamic, it would follow that there are educational consequences to these differences. Though the expected consequence of girls' lower achievement in schools is not widely evidenced, there is much validity indicating differential social consequences, which are, arguably, equally as significant. As McCormick and O'Connor suggest:

> Indeed, gender socialization theory hypothesizes that teachers' differential treatment of boys and girls may reinforce behaviors in children that reflect traditional relational styles. More specifically, girls are socialized to be compliant and behave responsibly, whereas compliant and responsible boys can be regarded as nonmasculine.[10]

Thus, there is a complex interaction between cultural behavioral expectations and perceptions of gender roles of even very young children as well as the importance of the teacher-child relationship. It is not surprising, then, that research suggests that when girls do not fit the gender profile (such as those who misbehave or do not achieve academically) and the teacher-child relationship is strained, girls tend to face more socially and academically harmful consequences as a result, such as lower academic achievement and growth.[11] Therefore, despite potential biological explanations, the research is becoming clearer that the social-emotional significance of the teacher-child relationship is closely related to actual schooling experience.

An applicable theory in social psychology known as *stereotype threat* serves a distinctly useful purpose in potentially understanding the propagation of these socially affected, if not socially learned interactions between girls and young women with their teachers. *Stereotype threat* is defined as "being at risk of confirming, as self-characteristic, a negative stereotype about one's group."[12] More specifically:

> When a stereotype about one's group indicts an important ability, one's performance in situations where that ability can be judged comes under extra pressure—that of possibly being judged by or self-fulfilling the stereotype—and this extra pressure may interfere with test performance.[13]

Given the social awareness that young women have of their gender-based cultural expectations, even at a young age, this phenomenon can help frame the propagation of gender inequality in schools.

It is important, however, to include aspects of the counter-narrative to this issue. That is, that some research supports that boys are actually more disadvantaged based on their gender in school than are girls.[14] Logic for this argument is based in the notion, supported even by the research that concludes that gender inequality is more significant in academic and social disadvantage of girls, that in general boys receive worse grades, get lower scores in reading assessments (especially at the elementary level), and are less likely to graduate high school than are girls.[15] This has led some researchers and advocates to declare a "boys' crisis" in education, with some even insinuating that this crisis has come about as a result of the increasing attention to girls' achievement, which they claim has come at the expense of boys.[16]

Indeed, some of the inconclusiveness of the findings in research is likely due to methodological limitations of the studies themselves. It appears that many of the studies implemented to investigate gender differences and gender inequality were largely nonlongitudinal and used summative rather than formative measures, both of which threaten the generalizability of the findings.

The research has also been largely compartmentalized, attempting to isolate certain singular processes that may have implications on such differences from the social perspective such as teacher expectations, parent-beliefs, or teacher-child relationships as well as the biological and neurological perspective such as apparent differences in standardized intelligence and cognitive test scores. Few studies, if any, however, have been successful in finding more comprehensive potential explanations for these supposed gender differences. This inability has resulted in potentially overly simplistic explanations for a likely more complex and multifaceted phenomenon.[17]

In attempt to address these complexities, a robust and comprehensive longitudinal study was conducted by the American Association for University Women (AAUW). This study used data collected for over 35 years to investigate the state of girls and young women in American public schools over time. Out of this study came a number of findings that are likely to help future studies design more comprehensive research endeavors and explicate the details of the issue more clearly and convincingly.

First, as aforementioned briefly, despite the increased achievement of boys and girls, the AAUW study found that the improvement of girls did not come at the expense of that of boys, as a number of researchers and advocates have suggested. This was a direct contradiction to the criticism that education is a "zero-sum game," a notion that can and should be applied in all discussions involving schooling inequality. Second, inequality in school cannot be narrowed by individual characteristics, but rather must be looked at comprehensively and as interactional. Essentially, it is unlikely that only one facet of identity alone can account for social inequality. Rather, it is the complex social interactions that result from the collective aspects of one's identity that do, which is difficult to capture empirically.

As many issues in schooling, identity, and discrimination suggest, the interaction between social, biological, and cultural variables can be dizzyingly complex yet lead to clear outcomes. The issue of gender bears no exception, and the solution to these problems lay in the increased understanding of the schooling and education community as a whole.

NOTES

1. Myra Sadker and David Sadker, *Failing at Fairness: How America's Schools Cheat Girls.* New York: Simon and Schuster, 2010, 15.

2. Ibid., 8.

3. Thomas Jefferson, as cited by James Carpenter, "Thomas Jefferson and the Ideology of Democratic Schooling." *Democracy and Education,* 21 no. 2, (2013): 1–11.

4. Ibid.

5. Ibid.

6. Claudia Buchmann, Thomas DiPrete, and Anne McDaniel, "Gender Inequalities in Education." *Annual Review of Sociology,* 34, (August 2008): 319–337.

7. D.F. Halpern, J. Wai, and A. Saw, "A Psychobiosocial Model: Why Females Are Sometimes Greater Than and Sometimes Less Than Males in Math Achievement." In A.M. Gallagher and J.C. Kaufman (Eds.) *Gender Differences in Mathematics: An Integrative Psychological Approach.* Cambridge, UK: Cambridge University Press.

8. Buchmann et al., "A Psychosocial Model."

9. Meghan P. McCormick and Erin E. O'Connor. "Teacher—Child Relationship Quality and Academic Achievement in Elementary School: Does Gender Matter?" *Journal of Educational Psychology,* 107 no. 2, (2015): 502–516.

10. Ibid., 504.

11. Ibid.

12. Claude M. Steele and Joshua Aronson, "Stereotype threat and the intellectual test performance
of African Americans." *Journal of Personality and Social Psychology,* 69 no. 5, (1995): 797–811.

13. Steven J. Spencer, Claude M. Steele, and Diane M. Quinn, "Stereotype and Women's Math
Performance." *Journal of Experimental Social Psychology,* 35 (1999): 4–28.

14. Joseph Paul Robinson and Sarah Theule Lubienski, "The Development of Gender Achievement Gaps in Mathematics and Middle School: Examining Direct Cognitive Assessments and Teacher Ratings." *American Educational Research Journal,* 48 no. 2, 268–302.

15. Ibid.

16. American Association of University Women, "Where the Girls Are." Retrieved from http://www.aauw.org/research/where-the-girls-are/.

17. Robinson and Lubienski, "Gender Achievement."

Chapter 15

Vicious Circles in Education Reform

A Conclusion

The purpose of this polemic was to provide a comprehensive foundation upon which inequality and circular attempts at education reform by policymakers plague American education reform history. However, proffering detailed descriptions of potential solutions to such reform failures was not. To achieve such a capability would require not only a comprehensive discussion of historical issues, such as that proffered in the current work, but also the current cultural, social, and educational conditions of a protean, mercurial, and ever-globalizing society.

In that vein, what will be offered in this final section is both a concise review of the history of American education reform as well as the introduction of a number of topics for future discourse, ones that must be earnestly evaluated and scrutinized should real progress in the area of education reform ever be truly achieved in America.

As the history of policymakers' attempts is unraveled and explored from multiple perspectives, especially those interpretations offered by scholars in the area of social science research, it becomes quite apparent that neither new ideas nor new actions attempting education reform have been implemented despite several cycles of reform efforts. While there have been subtle changes in rhetoric and fluctuations in bipartisan support, especially contemporarily regarding the Common Core State Standards, the foundations of such change have remained almost entirely stagnant.

From the republic's inception in the 1770s through the blatant racially segregated systems of the 1800s and continuing until the mid-1950s with the Brown decision, the country's judicial and governmental system was, quite blatantly, unequal regarding race. After the Brown decision, though the legislative language was changed, the social processes were maintained. This foundation in inequality was aptly applied to any such nonhegemonic group including women, those of non-Anglo or Western origins (including Eastern European white immigrants), Jews, and people with disabilities, among a number of other categorical "others." Essentially, it was a republic of equality and representation for some and control and containment for others.

The concept of most social reform projects, then, including and especially that of education has always been implemented to achieve one main underlying goal: assimilation. While it is inarguable that America is, at its very founding, a country of immigrants, a clear standard was established from the very beginnings of the new republic. That is, though all who inhabited the new republic were welcome to stay here in one way or another, there was a higher order of prioritization ensconced in the functionality of the new "free" system.

This system dictated that there was to be maintained a clear division between the decision makers and the group referred to by Adams as "the beast": common people, as well as those deemed even "lower than" the common people such as slaves, free blacks, Native Americans, and women. Though cloaked in the notion of representation, an enclave of the power elite quite quickly emerged and set the nation on the course of "control" rather than "participation," which has developed and functioned in a number of different ways and through a number of different systems.[1]

As a result, the notion of inequality of the "other" (whoever the other may be) and control by the "power elite" became an inherent mechanism in virtually every system that extended from the new and developing government. Therefore, when schooling became a matter of public concern and, therefore, public support (mainly financially), the grip of inequality was merely reproduced in its very mechanics. Mann's nascent public schooling system was exemplary of this notion. Though deemed almost immediately as "public" and available to all children, it was more likely an implantation of the Protestant ethic into the very blood of the nascent system. That is, those "others" could become more cultured *through* education, allowing schools to become the epicenters of both cultural conversion (of those who were non-Protestant) as well as cultural maintenance, preserving the cultural hegemony of the Protestant white, that which was seen not only as correct, but inherently "American."

Though Mann's notion of "equal schooling" between races, whether integrated *or* segregated, was never quite realized, even within his own time, his sense of elitism and its resulting "cultural amelioration" were undoubtedly implanted. That is, despite the inherently racist and elitist foundation of his approach (i.e., "Protestantization") the notion has been continuously used, in one way or another, as a means to justify and even systematize the degradation, vilification, and segregation of children based on their "otherness."

These cloaked tendencies of assimilation became the foundation of the neoliberal social movement beginning in the 1960s that, in many ways, served to nurture the ever-growing intermixing of the private corporate world with public functions as well as to propagate the often tacit notion of inherent racism, sexism, ableism, ethnocentrism, and xenophobia. That is, the purpose of reform of any type is social melioration, which consists of bringing those who are not to the middle-class standard upward toward it. In this context, neoliberal social movements cloak their efforts in privatization as efforts of social reform, arguing for the use of private money to enrich depressed and socially destitute communities.

Those leaders who would typically be considered neoconservatives, such as Reagan, George H.W. Bush, and especially George W. Bush, capitalized on the same neoliberal notions, ever involving the private corporate world in the business of the public "good." This cross-ideological activity reinforces the notion that, ultimately, classism plays as integral a role in hegemony than ideology and politics.

The liberal-leaning social scientists of the 1950s, in their conceptualization of remediating the "culturally deprived" black child to justify increased services for the black community, also employed this socially neoliberal and racially based approach. Even the staunchly Democratic liberal Lyndon Johnson and his "Great Society" plan concretized the conceptualization of the "poor black" in need of charitable attention in order to bring him or herself to the standards of American society.

Perhaps the quintessential 20th-century liberal Bill Clinton employed concepts of racial differences in order to infuse money and regulation in the schooling of poor black children. Prototypical conservatives utilized much of the same logic, such as George H.W. Bush's America 2000, and his biological and political progeny George W. Bush's "game changing" effort *No Child Left Behind*, which famously set the "soft bigotry of low expectations" as its rallying cry.

Essentially, the issue in American schooling has little to do with money, with expectations, with accountability, or with the narrowing focus of the public or private sectors. It has primarily to do with the notion of assimilation and the preservation of the middle-class ethic as the key to a prosperous society, with the aforementioned issues such as money and accountability being the functionary outcomes of the larger assimilation narrative.

The reform efforts of all types implemented for the American schooling system, be they deemed as liberal efforts of greater aid from a "welfare" perspective or conservative efforts of accountability and tighter fiscal management (both of which are now virtually interchangeable and no longer divisible into conservative or liberal efforts) all employ the same common mistake: that all Americans are to be assimilated, and the schools are to be the venues for this assimilation to take place. While lip service has been paid to concepts such as multiculturalism, awareness, such as Black History Month and Women's History Month, and character education, these remain merely nods in the service of political correctness, rather than true efforts toward garnering a genuine and functional pluralistic society.

What then might a country that is ever-challenged with representations of multiple cultures and ideologies, and a cultural and economic system based on individual gain, profit, and economic distinction do to truly reform its system in a meaningful way? It is argued that the following elements must be handled in an earnest, honest, and truly democratic manner, should any such meaningful progress be made.

First, the position in which the institution of public education has found itself regarding its deep and incestuous ties with corporate entities must be addressed and remediated directly. More specifically, the nascent but quickly burgeoning "educational industry" which spans from curricular materials, to standardized testing, to teacher evaluation methodologies and charter schools, must be entirely disentangled from public policy and re-relegated to the private realm alone.

It has been unmistakably clear that the increasing regulations in the area of public school standards, such as the Common Core State Standards (CCSS), and the panoply of evaluations and curricular materials that have accompanied it have little, if anything, to do with genuine education reform and only with profiteering. This is clear by the multiple financial privileges, from both private and public institutions, that investors in this industry enjoy. Worse, the civil rights rhetoric used to support elements of this movement, specifically school choice, serves only to rhetorically validate a system that is steeped in the propagation of segregated and inequitable schools.[2-5] Until the true nature of the charter school and, ipso facto, the privatization movement is revealed and dismantled, true public education reform cannot possibly take place.

Second, the question of centralization versus decentralization of American public schools must be revisited and resolved. While the language of legislative policy maintains that local education agencies and state governments retain primary power over public schools, current legislative policies and actions have deeply challenged the reality of that notion despite maintaining its rhetoric. For example, Race to the Top, a competitive grant proffered through the American Reinvestment and Recovery Act (ARRA), was pedaled as a "kick-starter" of sorts for state education departments to implement reform and innovation in the area of school reform.

Closer scrutiny, however, reveals a far more neoliberal-based economic impetus. As an extension of Race to the Top, the stipulations of the grant ostensibly forced state education departments to adopt the CCSS and, therefore, all of the newly available commercial products that accompanied it, many of which come from publishers with close political ties to the federal government such as McGraw-Hill and the Educational Testing Service. Additionally, states were essentially mandated to raise legislative caps on charter school establishments in order to be considered. Indeed, all states who won monies from Race to the Top complied with both the CCSS and charter school stipulations, as well as a number of other dubious requirements. These mandates call both the role of the market as well as the power of the federal government deeply into question.[6,7]

Third, the role that teachers and educationists play in direct education reform decision-making processes must be increased. With the central focus of education reform centering on profiteering and opening markets for investment, the value of those who are truly expert in teaching and instruction have been marginalized, if not entirely excluded from any form of genuine input. Further, what little input teachers and educationists force into the discussion is often dismissed as union rhetoric, anti-accountability sentiment, and the result of a disingenuous special interest. While countries such as Finland and India include the sentiments and advisement of public intellectuals and experts directly into their policymaking and educational practices, America not only excludes it, but vilifies the attempts of these individuals to be a part of the process.[8,9]

Fourth, the notion of a citizen, and what the role of the citizen and his or her ultimate civic duty in a globalizing world culture is must be reexamined and redefined. In most cases, American education reform is predicated on the notion of global competitiveness and, ultimately, supremacy. That is, it is the role of the public education system to rebuild and retain the centrality of economic and commercial superiority of America. Failure to achieve this goal signals a failure in the greater education system which signals a general degradation of American culture. While the rhetoric of such ideas often encompasses the notion of global citizenship, the central message in all such statements centers on global competitiveness and economic dominance.

Though there is a strong sense of nationalism in this context, the role that nationalism plays in a globalizing world must also be re-assessed, and the role that the education system plays in this re-assessment and reformation is central to both the discussion as well as the success of the effort. An essential component of this element is the practice of culturally responsive pedagogical methods and school environments. Despite the tendency for the popular rhetoric to contextualize multicultural aspects of American culture as something to be celebrated, it is far more than celebration and recognition that is needed. Rather, a deep investment in culturally responsive programs not only validates the plurality of cultures on a general and specific level, but also incorporates their narratives into the curriculum itself as an effort to expand the dominant narrative itself.

Fifth, but in no way final, more direct and honest attention must be paid to conditions in black and Hispanic communities in both urban and suburban neighborhoods. The notion that America has entered a post-racial era signified by the election of a black president is preposterous, and to insist that any systematic racism that has existed in the past is now a veritable relic is to ignore one of the most foundational problems that America faces. The achievement gap is real, the economic gap is real, the value gap is real,[10] and the cultural dominance gap is real; what remains synthetic is the attempts, from both liberal and conservative vantages, that have been made to "rectify" these issues.

To date there have been virtually no substantive, truly socially just efforts to rebuild these communities; rather, efforts to lure its inhabitants "out of them" with temptations of economic and social success have been touted as legitimate attempts at social change. So long as the "school to prison" pipeline remains intact and the systematic degradation of these communities is perpetuated through empty and ill-intended "welfare" programs instead of those based on true empowerment, cultural respect, and legitimized local leadership, these gaps will remain.

Essentially, the history of American education reform is one that has been more of an attempt at assimilation, Americanization, and a means of preserving the value system of the middle class. While some intentions and efforts may have been genuine, it is clear that the main result of virtually all attempts at education reform thus far have been political maneuvers cloaked in social reformation terms. Indeed, the faith that America has in its school system is justified and remains the hallmark of a true democratic society. However, what society has allowed its most precious of public systems to become is deplorable, and without true reformation the future of America, as well as the role it plays in a globalizing society, is at stake. It is time for a new discussion on education: one based in earnestness, honesty, and historical realization and divorced from rhetoric, big money, and political charade.

NOTES

1. Gordon Wood, *The Idea of America: Reflections on the Birth of the United States*. New York: Penguin, 2012.

2. Valerie Strauss. (2015). "Why Hedge Funds Love Charter Schools." Retrieved from https://www.washingtonpost.com/news/answer-sheet/wp/2014/06/04/why-hedge-funds-love-charter-schools/.

3. Addison Wiggin (2013). "Charter School Gravy Train Runs Express to Fat City." Retrieved from http://www.forbes.com/sites/greatspeculations/2013/09/10/charter-school-gravy-train-runs-express-to-fat-city/#6f9dae3470e5.

4. Sandra Vergari, "The Politics of Charter Schools." Educational Policy, (2007) 21, no. 15–39.

5. Gary Miron, Jessica L. Urschel, William J. Mathis, and Elana Tornquist, "Schools Without Diversity: Education Management Organizations, Charter Schools, and the Demographic Stratification of the American School System." Boulder, CO: Education and the Public Interest Center & Education Policy Research Unit. Retrieved from http://files.eric.ed.gov/fulltext/ED509329.pdf.

6. Paul Manna and Laura Ryan, "Competitive Grants and Educational Federalism: President Obama's Race to the Top Program in Theory and Practice." *The Journal of Federalism,* 41 no. 3, (2011): 522–546.

7. Joe Onosko, "Race to the Top Leaves Children and Future Citizens Behind: The Devastating Effects of Centralization, Standardization, and High Stakes Accountability." *Democracy and Education,* 19 no. 2, (2011): 1–11.

8. Pasi Sahlberg, "Education Reform for Raising Economic Competitiveness." *Journal of Educational Change*, 7 no. 4, (2006): 259–287.

9. Prema Clarke, "Culture and Classroom Reform: The Case of the District Primary Project, India." *Comparative Education,* 39 no. 1, (2003): 27–44.

10. Glaude Jr., *Democracy in Black.*

Bibliography

American Association of University Women, "Where the Girls Are." Retrieved from http://www.aauw.org/research/where-the-girls-are/.

Artiles, Alfredo J., Robert Rueda, Jesus Jose Salazar, and Ignacio Higareda. "Within-Group Diversity in Minority Disproportionate Representation: English Language Learners in Urban School Districts." *Exceptional Children,* 71 no. 2, (2005): 283–300.

Artiles, Alfredo J., Beth Harry, Daniel J. Reschly, and Philip C. Chinn. "Overidentification of Students of Color in Special Education: A Critical Overview." *Multicultural Perspectives,* 4 no. 1, (2002): 3–10.

Ayers, Bill. *Public Enemy: Confessions of an American Dissident.* New York: Beacon, 2013.

Ayres, Leonard P. *Laggards in Our Schools: A Study of Retardation and Elimination in City School Systems.* New York: Charities, 1909.

Banks, James A. "Multicultural Education: Historical Development, Dimensions, and Practice." *Review of Research in Education,* 19, (1993): 3–49.

Baynton, Douglas. "Disability and the Justification of Inequality in American History." *Mental Retardation,* 40 no. 1, (2002): 51–55.

Bell, Derrick. "The Legacy of W.E.B. DuBois: A Rational Model for Achieving Public School Equity for America's Black Children." *Creighton Law Review,* 11 (1978): 409–431.

Delgado Bernal, Dolores. "Critical Race Theory, Latino Critical Theory, and Critical Raced-Gendered Epistomologies: Recognizing Students of Color as Holders and Creators of Knowledge." *Qualitative Inquiry,* 8 no. 1, (2002): 105–126.

Boake, Corwin. "From the Binet-Simon to the Wechsler-Bellevue: Tracing the History of Intelligence Testing." *Journal of Clinical and Experimental Neuropsychology,* 24 no. 3, (2002): 383–405.

Bohon, Stephanie A., Heather Macpherson, and Jorge H. Atiles. (2005). "Educational Barriers for New Latinos in Georgia." *Journal of Latinos and Education,* 4 no. 1, (2005): 43–58.

Bonilla-Silva, Eduardo. "We are All Americans!: The Latin Americanization of Racial Stratification in the USA." *Race & Society*, 5, (2002): 3–16.

Bonilla-Silva, Eduardo. *White Supremacy and Racism in the Post-Civil Rights Era.* Lynne Rienner Publishers: Boulder, CO, 2001.

Platt Bouston, Leah. "Was Postwar Suburbanization White flight? Evidence from the Black Migration." *The Quarterly Journal of Economics,* 125 no. 1, (2010): 417–443.

Bracey, Gerald W. "April Foolishness: The 20th Anniversary of a Nation at Risk" *Phi Delta Kappan*, 84 no. 8, (2003): 616–621.

Buchmann, Claudia, Thomas DiPrete, and Anne McDaniel. "Gender Inequalities in Education." *Annual Review of Sociology*, 34, (August 2008): 319–337.

Carpenter, James. "Thomas Jefferson and the Ideology of Democratic Schooling." *Democracy and Education,* 21 no. 2, (2013): 1–11.

Carter, Launor F. (1984). "The Sustaining Effects Study of Compensatory and Elementary Education." *Educational Researcher*, 13 no. 7, (1984): 4–13.

Clarke, Prema. "Culture and Classroom Reform: The Case of the District Primary Project, India." *Comparative Education,* 39 no. 1, (2003): 27–44.

Chomsky, Noam. Hegemony or Survival: America's Quest for Global Dominance. New York: Holt, 2004.

Cole, Michael, Vera John-Steiner, Sylvia Scribner, and Ellen Souberman (Eds.). Mind in society: The development of higher psychological processes. Cambridge, MA: Harvard University Press, 1980.

Coleman, James S. "Recent Trends in School Integration," *Educational Researcher*, 4 no. 7, (1975): 3–12.

Conchas, Gilberto Q. "Structuring Failure and Success: Understanding the Variability in Latino School Engagement." *Harvard Educational Review*, 71 no. 3, (2001): 475.

Dewey, John. *Democracy and Education*. New York: Free Press, 1916/1997.

Edley, Christopher E. "Introduction: Lawyers and Education Reform." *Harvard Journal on Legislation* 28, (1991): 293.

Eitel, Robert S. and Kent D. Talbert. "The Road to a National Curriculum: The Legal Aspects of the Common Core State Standards, Race to the Top, and Conditional Waivers." *Engage*, 13 no. 1, (2012): 13–25.

Eitle, Tamela McNulty. "Special Education or Racial Segregation: Understanding Variation in the Representation of Black Students in Educable Mentally Handicapped Programs." *The Sociological Quarterly,* 43 no. 4, (2002): 575–605.

Farlie, Robert Q., and Alexandra M. Resch. "Is There 'White flight' into Private Schools? Evidence from the National Educational Longitudinal Survey." *The Review of Economics and Statistics*, 84 no. 1, (2002): 21–33.

Fasko Jr., Daniel. (2001). "An Analysis of Multiple Intelligences Theory and its Use with the Gifted and Talented." *Roeper Review*, 23 no. 3, (2001): 127–130.

Frankenberg, Erika, Chungmei Lee, and Gary Orfield (2003). "A Multicultural Society with Segregated Schools: Are We Losing the Dream?" From http://escholarship.org/uc/item/3rh7w18g#page-1.

Frey, William H. "Central City White flight: Racial and Nonracial Causes." *American Sociological Review,* 44 no. 3, (1979): 425–448.

Frey, William H. (1979) "Black In-Migration, White flight, and the Changing Economic Base of the Central City." *American Journal of Sociology*, 85 no. 6, (1979): 1396–1417.

Gallagher, Ann M., and James C. Kaufman (Eds.) *Gender Differences in Mathematics: An Integrative Psychological Approach.* Cambridge, UK: Cambridge University Press, 2005.

Glaude, Jr., Eddie S. *Democracy in Black: How Race Still Enslaves the American Soul.* New York: Crown Publishers, 2015.

Gould, Stephen Jay. *The Mismeasure of Man.* New York: W.W. Norton & Co., 1996.

Gravois, Todd A. and Sylvia A. Rosenfield. (2006). "Impact of Instructional Consultation Teams on the Disproportionate Referral and Placement of Minority Students in Special Education." *Remedial and Special Education,* 27 no. 1, (2006): 42–52.

Gregory, Robert J. *Psychological Testing: History, Principles, and Applications (6th ed.)* New York: Allyn & Bacon, 2011.

Harris, Cheryl I. "Whiteness as Property." *Harvard Law Review*, 106, (1993): 1721.

Harry, Beth and Janette Klingner. "Discarding the Deficit Model." *Educational Leadership,* 64 no. 5, (2007): 16–21.

Hehir, Thomas. "Confronting Ableism." *Educational Leadership*, 64 no. 5, (2007): 8–14.

Hehir, Thomas. Eliminating ableism in education. *Harvard Educational Review,* 72, (2002): 1–32.

Henretta, James A. "Families and Farms: Mentalité in Pre-Industrial America." *The William & James Quarterly,* 35 no. 1, (1980): 3–32.

Hiser, Elizabeth and Carl Francis. "Intelligence: A Brief History." *Journal of Inquiry and Research*, 72, (2000).

Hoyt, Homer. "The Relation of a Literacy Test to a Constructive Immigration Problem." *Journal of Political Economy,* 24 no. 5, (1916): 445–473.

Katz, Michael B. "The Origins of Public Education: A Reassessment." *History of Education Quarterly*, 16 no. 4, (1976): 381–407.

Kliebard, Herbert M. *The Struggle for the American Curriculum, 1893–1958.* New York: Routledge, 2004.

Klinginger, Janette K., and Beth Harry. "The Special Education Referral and Decision-Making Process for English Language Learners: Child Study Team Meetings and Staffings." *Teachers College Record, 108*, (2006): 2247–2281.

Klinginger, Janette K., Alfredo J. Artiles, Elizabeth Kozelski et al. (2005). "Addressing the Disproportionate Representation of Culturally and Linguistically Diverse Students in Special Education through Culturally Responsive Educational Systems." *Education Policy Analysis Archives,* 13 no. 38, (2005). Retrieved from http://epaa.asu.edu/epaa/v13m38.

Kruse, Kevin M. *One Nation Under God: How Corporate America Invented Christian America.* New York: Basic Books, 2015.

Kumasi, Kafi D. (2011). Critical Race Theory and Education: Mapping a Legacy of Scholarship and Activism." In Levinson, B.A.U. (Ed.), Beyond Critique: Critical Social Theories and Education (pp. 196–219). Boulder, CO: Paradigm Publishers.

Ladson-Billings, Gloria. "Just what is Critical Race Theory and What's it Doing in a *Nice* Field Like Education?" *Qualitative Studies in Education,* 11 no. 1, (1996): 7–24.

Longmore, Paul K., and Lauri Umanski. *The New Disability History: American Perspectives.* New York: NYU Press, 2001.

Lourenco, Orlando and Armanda Machado. "In Defense of Piaget's Theories: A Reply to 10 Common Criticisms." *Psychological Review,* 103 no. 1, (1997): 143–164.

Manna, Paul and Laura Ryan. "Competitive Grants and Educational Federalism: President Obama's Race to the Top Program in Theory and Practice." *The Journal of Federalism,* 41 no. 3, (2011): 522–546.

McCarthy, Cameron. "Rethinking Liberal and Radical Perspectives on Racial Equality in Schooling: Making the Case for Nonsynchrony." *Harvard Educational Review,* 58 (1988): 3.

McCormick, Meghan P., and Erin E. O'Connor. "Teacher—Child Relationship Quality and Academic Achievement in Elementary School: Does Gender Matter?" *Journal of Educational Psychology,* 107 no. 2, (2015): 502–516.

Miron, Gary, Jessica L. Urschel, William J. Mathis, and Elana Tornquist. (2010). "Schools Without Diversity: Education Management Organizations, Charter Schools, and the Demographic Stratification of the American School System." Boulder, CO: Education and the Public Interest Center & Education Policy Research Unit. Retrieved from http://files.eric.ed.gov/fulltext/ED509329.pdf.

Mondale, Sarah. *School: The Story of American Public Education.* New York: Beacon, 2002.

Neisser, Ulric et al. "Intelligence: Knowns and Unknowns." American Psychologist, 51, no. 2, (1996): 77–101.

Nolen, Jennifer L. Multiple Intelligences in the Classroom. *Education,* 124 no. 1, (2003): 115–119.

Ogbu, John U., and Herbert D. Simons (1998). "Voluntary and Involuntary Minorities: A Cultural-Ecological Theory of School Performance with Some Implications for Education." *Anthropology & Education Quarterly,* 29 no. 2, (1998): 55–188.

Ogbu, John U. "Racial Stratification and Education in the United States: Why Inequality Persists." *Teachers College Record,* 96 no. 2, (1994): 264–298.

Omi, Michael and Howard Winant. *Racial Formation in the United States from the 1960s to the 1990s.* New York: Routledge, 1994.

Onosko, Joe. "Race to the Top Leaves Children and Future Citizens Behind: The Devastating Effects of Centralization, Standardization, and High Stakes Accountability." *Democracy and Education,* 19 no. 2, (2011): 1–11.

Orfield, Gary. Reviving the Goal of an Integrated Society: A 21st Century Challenge, 2009. From http://escholarship.org/uc/item/2bw2s608#page-13.

Paneque, Oneyda M., and Patricia M. Barbetta. "A Study of Teacher Efficacy of Special Education Teachers of English Language Learners with Disabilities." *Bilingual Research Journal,* 30 no. 1, (2006): 171–193.

Pervin, Lawrence A. *Goal Concepts in Personality and Social Psychology.* New York: Psychology Press, 2015.

Porter, Andrew, Jennifer McMaken, Jun Hwang, and Rui Yang. "Common Core State Standards: The New U.S. Intended Curriculum." *Educational Researcher,* 40 no. 3, (2011): 103–116.

Postman, Neil. *The End of Education: Redefining the Value of School.* New York: Vintage, 1996.

Rauscher, Laura and Mary McClintock. Ableism curriculum design. In M. Adams, L.A. Bell, and P. Griffen (Eds.) Teaching for Diversity and Social Justice (pp. 198–231). New York: Routledge, 1996.

Ravitch, Diane. *The Troubled Crusade: American Education 1945–1980.* New York: Basic Books, 1985.

Richardson, Ken. "What IQ Tests Test." Theory & Psychology, 12 no. 3, (2002): 283–314.

Robinson, Joseph Paul and Sarah Theule Lubienski (2011). "The Development of Gender Achievement Gaps in Mathematics and Middle School: Examining Direct Cognitive Assessments and Teacher Ratings." *American Educational Research Journal*, 48 no. 2, 268–302.

Roselli, Monca and Alfredo Ardila. "The Impact of Culture and Education on Non-Verbal Neuropsychological Measurements: A Critical Review." *Brain and Cognition*, 52, (2003): 326–333.

Roth, Michael S. *Beyond the University: Why Liberal Education Matters.* New Haven, CT: Yale University Press, 2015.

Rothstein, Richard. "A Nation at Risk Twenty-Five Years Later." CATO Unbound. (2005): Retrieved from http://www.cato-unbound.org/2008/04/07/richard-rothstein/nation-risk-twenty-five-years-later.

Sadker, Myra and David Sadker. *Failing at Fairness: How America's Schools Cheat Girls.* New York: Simon and Schuster, 2010.

Sahlberg, Pasi. "Education Reform for Raising Economic Competitiveness." *Journal of Educational Change*, 7 no. 4, (2006): 259–287.

Shuttleworth-Edwards, Ann B., Ryan D. Kemp, Annegret L. Rust et al. "Cross-cultural Effects on IQ Test Performance: A Review and Preliminary Normative Indications on the WAIS-III Test Performance." *Journal of Clinical and Experimental Neuropsychology,* 26 no. 7, (2004): 903–920.

Shyman, Eric. *Beyond Equality in the American Classroom: The Case for Inclusive Education.* Lanham, MD: Lexington Books, 2013.

Skiba, Russell, Ada Simmons, Shana Ritter et al. "The Context of Minority Disproportionality: Practitioner Perspectives on Special Education Referral." *Teachers College Record,* 108 no. 7, (2006): 1424–1459.

Skiba, Russell, Ada B. Simmons, Shanna Ritter, Ashley Gibb, M. Karega Rausch, Jason Cuadrado, and Choong-Geun Chung. "Achieving Equity in Special Education: History, Status, and Current Challenges." *Exceptional Children,* 74 no. 3, (2008): 264–288.

Sokol, Jason. *All Eyes are Upon Us: Race and Politics from Boston to Brooklyn.* New York: Basic Books, 2015.

Spencer, Steven J., Claude M. Steele, and Diane M. Quinn. "Stereotype and Women's Math Performance." *Journal of Experimental Social Psychology*, 35, (1999): 4–28.

Steele, Claude M., and Joshua Aronson. (1995). "Stereotype threat and the intellectual test performance of African Americans." *Journal of Personality and Social Psychology*, 69 no. 5, (1995): 797–811.

Steele, Shelby. *Shame: How America's Past Sins Have Polarized our Country.* New York: Basic Books, 2015.

Sternberg, Robert J., and Elena L. Grigorenko. "Intelligence and Culture: How Culture Shapes What Intelligence Means, and the Implications for a Science of Well-Being." *Philosophical Transactions of the Royal Society of London,* 359, (2004): 1427–1434.

Sullivan, Amanda. "Disproportionality in Special Education Identification and Placement of English Language Learners." *Exceptional Children,* 77 no. 3, (2011): 317–334.

Trent, James W. *Inventing the Feeble Mind: A History of Mental Retardation in the United States.* Los Angeles: University of California Press, 1995.

Tucker, Carl M., Terrence Porter, Wendy M. Reinke et al. "Promoting Teacher Efficacy for Working with Culturally Diverse Students." *Preventing School Failure,* 50 no. 1, (2005): 29–34.

Tyack, David and Larry Cuban. *Tinkering Toward Utopia: A Century of Public School Reform.* Cambridge, MA: Harvard University Press, 1997.

Sandra Vergari, "The Politics of Charter Schools." Educational Policy, (2007) 21, no. 15–39.

Vittieri, Joseph P. *Choosing Equality: School Choice, the Constitution, and Civil Society.*

Washington, D.C.: Brookings Institution Press, 2012.

Wallace Wallin, J. E. *The Education of Handicapped Children* (New York: Houghton Mifflin, 1924), 92–93.

Wood, Gordon. *The Idea of America: Reflections on the Birth of the United States.* New York: Penguin, 2012.

Woodson, Carter G. "Negro Life and History in our Schools." *The Journal of Negro History,* 4 no. 3, (1919): 273–280.

Zigmond, Naomi. "Where Should Students with Disabilities Receive Special Education Services?" *The Journal of Special Education,* 37 no. 3, (2003): 193–199.

About the Author

Eric Shyman is assistant professor of child study at St. Joseph's College in New York. He earned his doctorate degree from Teachers College, Columbia University, in 2009.